EVENTS
THAT CHANGED THE WORLD

Bounty
Books

An Hachette UK Company
www.hachette.co.uk

Published in Great Britain in 2018 by Bounty Books,
a division of Octopus Publishing Group Ltd
Carmelite House, 50 Victoria Embankment, London EC4Y 0DZ
www.octopusbooks.co.uk

ISBN 978-0-7537-3292-2

A CIP catalogue record for this book is available from the British Library

Printed and bound in China

10 9 8 7 6 5 4 3 2 1

For the Bounty edition
Publisher: Lucy Pessell
Designer: Lisa Layton
Editor: Sarah Vaughan
Production Controller: Sarah Kulasek-Boyd

EVENTS
THAT CHANGED THE WORLD

CONTENTS

HUMANITY
AND LIBERTY

Emmeline Pankhurst Imprisoned

Gandhi's Imprisonment

Rosa Parks' Bus Protest

The Paris Student Protests

Nelson Mandela Released from Prison

EMMELINE PANKHURST IMPRISONED

JULY 16, 1872–JUNE 18, 1928

"Men make the moral code and they expect women to accept it. They have decided that it is entirely right and proper for men to fight for their liberties and their rights, but that it is not right and proper for women to fight for theirs."

Emmeline Pankhurst on the importance of the suffragette cause.

Born to activist parents, Pankhurst become a self-confessed suffragette at the age of 14 but didn't became an activist until after her marriage to Richard Pankhurst in 1897. Richard Pankhurst was a lawyer who had formed the National Society for Women's Suffrage and was the author of the 1882 Married Women's Act, which gave wives control over their own money. He supported Emmeline in her suffragette struggle and helped her found the Women's Franchise League, which aimed to win women the right to vote in local elections. Richard's death in 1889 was a great blow to Emmeline and she was forced to bring up their five children alone.

On March 4, 1912, Emmeline Pankhurst's Women's Social and Political Union (WSPU) wrought havoc in central London by smashing shop windows in the West End and attacking government buildings. The increasingly militant behavior of the WSPU reached fever pitch in 1913, when suffragette Emily Davison was killed after throwing herself in front of the king's horse at the Epsom Derby. Jail authorities, who at first had resorted to force-feeding suffragettes on hunger strikes, changed their policy after the Cat and Mouse Act allowed hunger-striking prisoners to be freed and then rearrested after regaining their health.

At the outbreak of the First World War, Emmeline Pankhurst urged women in Britain to give up the suffragette fight so they could help with the war effort. She traveled to the United States, Canada and Russia to encourage the mobilization of women and lived in the United States after the war. After admitting to the valuable contribution made by women during the war, the British government passed the Representation of the People Act 1918, which gave women over the age of 30 the right to vote.

After the war, Pankhurst was still an advocate for women's rights and an ardent suffragette, but she no longer advocated the militant approach. When parliament passed a law allowing women to become ministers of parliament, Pankhurst worked tirelessly on her daughter Christabel's campaign – although in the end she was not elected. In March 1928, the British government introduced the Representation of the People (Equal Franchise) Act to give women the same voting rights as men. The bill became law in July, a few weeks after Emmeline Pankhurst's death.

❧

In 1908, Emmeline Pankhurst was imprisoned after trying to invade parliament to present a petition to British prime minister H.H. Asquith. Never one to sit quietly, the suffragette leader railed loudly against her six-week confinement and the rats, the meagre meals and the "civilized torture of solitary confinement and absolute silence" that she was made to endure. It would not be Pankhurst's only spell inside: she was imprisoned 14 times for her activities in the Women's Social and Political Union (WSPU), an organization she founded in 1903 to win women the vote. Pankhurst advised the members of the WSPU, known as the "suffragettes", that direct action was needed to bring about a change of government policy. "Deeds not words, was to be our permanent motto," Pankhurst later wrote.

The WSPU's early activities took non-violent forms that included rallies, speeches and petitions, but its methods changed when a 1905 bill for women's suffrage was rejected in parliament. Standing outside the Houses of Parliament, members of the WSPU began to protest loudly at the news and had to be forcibly removed by police. The publicity caused by the protest gave Pankhurst the idea to adopt a more militant approach. From that point on, the WSPU pursued measures that included violent demonstrations, window smashing, arson and hunger strikes.

The behavior was considered highly unfeminine and unseemly, especially for Pankhurst herself, a mother of five. The police often retaliated aggressively to the WSPU protests, reportedly punching protesters and pulling their breasts during one particularly heated march. The campaign of violence, however, did not last. Pankhurst halted the suffrage activities at the outbreak of the First World War, so that her WSPU members could join the war effort. The contribution of women during the war encouraged several countries to grant them the vote. In Britain this came about in 1928, the year of Pankhurst's death.

—◦◦◇◦◦—

A Timeline: the Life, Experience and Influence of Emmeline Pankhurst

1867 John Stuart Mill raises the issue of women's suffrage in the British House of Commons.

1889 Emmeline and Richard Pankhurst form the Women's Franchise League.

1893 New Zealand becomes the first nation in the world to give women the vote.

1897 The National Union of Women's Suffrage Societies (NUWSS) is formed.

1904 The International Women Suffrage Alliance is founded in Berlin.

1907 A Women's Social and Political Union (WSPU) breakaway group, The Women's Freedom League, is formed.

1909 The WSPU introduces violent tactics to further its cause.

1913 The WSPU begins its national arson campaign.

1913 The Cat and Mouse Act is passed, permitting the release of hunger-striking suffragettes from prison and their rearrest after they had started eating.

1913 U.S. suffragette organization the Feminist Congressional Union begins a campaign of civil disobedience and pickets the White House to publicize its cause.

1913 Norway gives women the vote.

1914 Emmeline Pankhurst calls for the cessation of suffragette activities as war breaks out.

1916 Manitoba becomes the first Canadian province to give women the vote.

1918 Christabel Pankhurst stands in the British general election as the Women's Party candidate for Smethwick, although she is narrowly beaten.

1918 The British Representation of the People Act gives the vote to women over 30 who "occupy premises of a yearly value of not less than £5".

1920 The U.S. Senate passes the Nineteenth Amendment, prohibiting state or federal sex-based restrictions on voting in America.

1928 The British Representation of the People Act gives women the same voting rights as men.

1976 Portugal gives women the same voting rights as men.

1984 The European state of Liechtenstein gives women the vote.

GANDHI'S IMPRISONMENT

1930

"I object to violence because when it appears
to do good, the good is only temporary;
the evil it does is permanent."

Mohandas "Mahatma" Gandhi explains his advocacy of non-violence.

After the British government failed to address calls to give India dominion status, Gandhi struck out on his first salt march in 1930. Under British law, it was illegal for Indians to collect or refine salt. In defiance of this law Gandhi walked 386km (240 miles) to the sea, where he gathered a handful of salt. Huge crowds came to support Gandhi in this non-violent action and the rattled British government imprisoned over 60,000 people in response.

Gandhi's salt march encouraged many others to follow his example and disobey the law on salt, which led to Gandhi's arrest and imprisonment for a second salt march in 1930. As a result of the unrest, Gandhi was invited to London in 1931 to discuss Indian self-rule with British ministers. Known as the Round Table Conference, the talks failed after agreement could not be reached between the British government and the attending Hindu and Muslim representatives. A disappointed Gandhi returned to India to continue the fight for independence.

The Quit India campaign, launched by Gandhi and Indian National Congress leader Jawaharlal Nehru in 1942, was designed to disrupt the British war effort through Indian civil disobedience. It called for the immediate withdrawal of Britain from India. The campaign garnered great support among Indians, who staged strikes and carried out acts of sporadic violence across the country. The British government reacted by arresting nearly the whole of the Indian National Congress leadership and keeping them imprisoned until 1945. Without clear leadership, the Quit India campaign was quickly crushed by the British army. However, the campaign showed Britain that its ongoing governance of India was untenable.

In 1946, sectarian violence erupted after India's Muslim League party demanded a separate homeland for Muslims as part of a deal for Indian independence. This led to Indian Viceroy Lord Louis Mountbatten's 1947 announcement that India would be partitioned into separate states for Hindus and Muslims. The result was the displacement of millions of Muslims and Hindus on the day of independence, as the separate nations of India and Pakistan were formed. The region of Punjab was split between these two countries, resulting in religious rioting and genocide, and the deaths of hundreds of thousands of people.

The Second World War marked the turning point in Mohandas "Mahatma" Gandhi's campaign to end British rule in India. The leader of the Indian National Congress and advocate of non-violent resistance, Gandhi could not tolerate a war that would conscript thousands of Indians into the British army. After launching a program of civil disobedience in 1930, Gandhi now endorsed a new "Quit India" campaign, which put the country on the road to freedom.

Gandhi had begun his struggle for Indian independence after fighting against racial prejudice as a lawyer in South Africa. On his return in 1915 he called on his countrymen to seek independence from Britain through non-violent means. Gandhi put his methods into action after Britain broke its promise to free India after the First World War.

Gandhi's early acts of passive resistance included the boycott of foreign textiles, but after the Amritsar massacre of 1919 he launched the new "Non-Co-operation Movement". Gandhi's arrest for his salt marches in 1930 sparked large protests, and tens of thousands were arrested after marching in the streets. Gandhi's 1930 imprisonment was only one of many. His last jail term came in 1942, when Gandhi and his fellow leaders were arrested just hours after launching their Quit India campaign and imprisoned without trial for two years. The Quit India campaign went ahead, but without Gandhi's guidance many of his followers resorted to violent methods, including the sabotage of railway and telegraph lines and the use of bombs.

Realizing their days of rule in India were over, the British granted India independence in 1947. However, this resulted in the partition of India to form Pakistan, which led to violence and genocide and left India splintered and brutalized. Gandhi was assassinated by a Hindu extremist in 1948. Today, Gandhi is considered the father of India and his name is forever linked with the civil-rights movement and the fight against oppression.

———◦◦◦◦◦———

A Timeline: the Life, Experience and Influence of Gandhi

1915 Gandhi returns to India after spending 21 years as a barrister in South Africa.

1917 Gandhi launches the Non-Co-operation campaign of satyagraha, formed from the Sanskrit words for "truth" and "firmness".

1919 British soldiers kill 379 protesters during the Amritsar massacre in the Punjab region.

1922 Gandhi calls for a boycott on imported textiles, which were damaging India's own textile industries. Gandhi encourages Indians to wear home-woven cloth, and dresses himself in simple white clothes, sandals and spectacles.

May 1930 Following Gandhi's imprisonment, tens of thousands of his followers are arrested and incarcerated.

1930 Women across India follow Gandhi's salt march protest by illegally boiling sea water to make salt.

1931 After the failed Round Table Conference talks in London, Gandhi visits Lancashire mill workers, who have been affected by the Indian boycott of foreign cloth.

1934 Gandhi launches the All-India Village Industries Association.

1934 Gandhi becomes a champion of the Untouchables, the lowest caste in Indian society.

1935 The Government of India Act grants Indian provinces power over local administrative affairs.

1939 Britain declares war on Germany on India's behalf, without consulting leaders of its own parties. Over 2.5 million Indian soldiers fight during the war.

1940 In opposition to the Indian National Congress, the Muslim League comes out in support of Britain's part in the Second World War.

1942 Indian workers go on strike as part of Gandhi's "Quit India" campaign.

1946 Over 4,000 people are killed as sectarian violence between Muslims and Hindus breaks out in Calcutta.

1947 Millions of Indians find themselves displaced as partition comes into force during the independence of India.

1947 Jawaharlal Nehru becomes the first prime minister of India.

1947 Between 200,000 and 500,000 people are killed during the genocide in Punjab.

1948 Mahatma Gandhi is shot dead on January 30 on his way to pray.

1948 Muhammad Ali Jinnah becomes Pakistan's first governor general.

ROSA PARKS' BUS PROTEST

1955

"I'd see the bus pass every day...but to me, that was a way of life; we had no choice but to accept what was the custom. The bus was among the first ways I realized there was a black world and a white world."

Rosa Parks remembers seeing the bus for white children drive past as she walked to school.

On December 5, 1955 – four days after Rosa Parks was arrested – a black boycott of Montgomery buses was called for. Members of the National Association for the Advancement of Colored People (NAACP) handed out tens of thousands of handbills, church leaders told their congregations to stay off the buses and a front-page article in the Montgomery Advertiser spread the word around Montgomery. It was agreed that black people would stay off the buses until segregation had been removed, black drivers had been hired and black people were treated with same courtesy on buses as whites. Over 40,000 black commuters stayed off the buses the next morning, choosing to walk, ride in carpools or travel in black-operated cabs that charged them ten cents – the same fare as on the bus.

Following the civil disobedience sparked by the Montgomery bus boycott, four university students staged a sit-in at a Woolworths store in Greensboro, North Carolina. After shopping at Woolworths, the university men were refused service at the store's segregated lunch counter. Despite being asked to leave, the four students stayed at the counter until the store closed. The next day, over 20 black students staged another sit-in, and the following day over 60 more. The protest soon spread to other towns in North Carolina and then the neighboring states of Mississippi, Virginia, Kentucky and Tennessee. The protests proved to be a pivotal moment in the American civil-rights movement and led to President Dwight D. Eisenhower expressing his sympathy for the cause. The Greensboro Woolworths store changed its segregation policy soon afterwards.

On August 28, 1962, over 200,000 protestors gathered for a civil-rights rally known as "the March on Washington for Jobs and Freedom". The march was designed to draw attention to the growing dissatisfaction over black discrimination in America, and culminated in Martin Luther King, Jr.'s "I Have a Dream" speech, which called for economic and political equality. In addition to Martin Luther King, Jr., the march included performances by Joan Baez and Bob Dylan and was broadcast live on television, which brought great publicity to the civil-rights cause.

From the mid-1960s, the American federal government passed a number of laws banning racial discrimination in the United States: the Civil Rights Act of 1964 outlawed discrimination based on race, color, religion, sex or national origin; the Voting Rights Act of 1965 prohibited racial discrimination in voting; and the Fair Housing Act of 1968 made it illegal to discriminate racially when selling or renting property. While serious issues concerning racial inequality remain in America to the present day, the civil-rights movement that had been ignited by Rosa Parks in 1955 was pivotal in securing equal rights by law.

Rosa Parks seemed like an ordinary Montgomery seamstress going about her everyday life when she boarded her bus home on December 1, 1955. But through a simple and quiet moment of civil disobedience, she was about to change history.

Buses in Alabama at that time were segregated into sections for whites and blacks, and Parks sat down just behind the ten seats reserved for whites. When the bus filled with white people, Parks was obliged to move – but she refused to stand up. The bus driver threatened to call the police, and then did so when this did not have the desired effect. Parks was duly arrested, fingerprinted and charged with violating the segregation laws, commonly known as the "Jim Crow Laws". Parks appealed against her conviction and challenged the legality of segregation under the American Constitution. As she did so, little-known civil-rights leader Martin Luther King, Jr. initiated a boycott of Montgomery buses by black Americans, who made up around 70 percent of its passengers.

Nearly a year later, on November 13,1956, the U.S. Supreme Court upheld a lower court's decision that Montgomery's segregated buses were unconstitutional. A court order to this effect was served the next day and the bus boycott officially ended on December 20. The ruling was a monumental moment in American history that ignited the civil-rights movement across the country. The boycott brought Martin Luther King, Jr. to prominence and made Rosa Parks famous as the "mother of the civil-rights movement". Parks was not viewed with the same admiration by her employers. She was fired from her job and had to leave Montgomery after being unable to obtain work. She was later employed as a secretary for a U.S. congressman in Michigan and co-founded the Rosa and Raymond Parks Institute for Self Development, which gave career advice to young people, against oppression.

—◦◦◦◦◦—

A Timeline: the Life, Experience and Influence of Rosa Parks

1865 The Thirteenth Amendment formally outlaws slavery in the United States.

1876 The American southern states pass the first Jim Crow Laws.

1909 The National Negro Committee is formed, which will become the National Association for the Advancement of Colored People (NAACP).

1914 Newly elected, President Woodrow Wilson orders resegregation of federal workplaces.

1925 Over 35,000 Ku Klux Klan members march in Washington, DC.

1942 The Congress of Racial Equality (CORE) is established.

1954 The U.S. Supreme Court declares segregation in schools to be unconstitutional.

1955 The Montgomery bus boycott begins after the arrest of Rosa Parks.

1957 President Dwight D. Eisenhower orders federal troops to enforce the law that black students can attend Little Rock High School in Arkansas.

1960 The first student sit-ins against segregation at North Carolina lunch counters begin.

1962 Federal troops are ordered in to protect black student James Meredith's right to attend Mississippi University.

1963 Over 200,000 civil-rights protesters march in Washington.

1964 Martin Luther King, Jr. is awarded the Nobel Peace Prize.

1965 Civil-rights leader Malcolm X is assassinated.

1965 Martin Luther King, Jr. leads the civil-rights march from Selma to Montgomery, Alabama.

1965 Thirty-four people are left dead after violent race riots in Watts, Los Angeles.

1967 State laws forbidding interracial marriage are declared unconstitutional by the Supreme Court.

1968 Martin Luther King, Jr. is assassinated.

THE PARIS STUDENT PROTESTS

1968

"I greet the year 1968 with serenity. It is impossible
to see how France today could be paralyzed by
crisis as she has been in the past."

French President Charles de Gaulle broadcasts his annual New
Year message to the nation.

After protests at the Sorbonne's Nanterre campus erupted in March,
the police arrested four of its students, the first of many over the
following months. On this occasion, the students had been staging an
anti-Vietnam War rally, although many other protests were also held.
Often the students demonstrated against substandard conditions on
campus, as well as an education system they believed was outdated
and inadequately funded. After the arrests several hundred students,
who later formed the Mouvement du 22 Mars ("Movement of 22
March"), stormed the university buildings. This action, in part, led to
the police closure of the Sorbonne on May 2. After the riots of May 6,
a huge crowd congregated on Paris's Left Bank on May 10.

After the police blocked the protestors from crossing the river, clashes once again broke out as the crowd knocked over the barricades that had been erected to contain them. The street riots lasted until dawn the next day and the injuries and arrests were once again broadcast on television to viewers around the world. Many of the protestors alleged agents provocateurs had been employed by the government to throw Molotov cocktails and burn cars. The police brutality that occurred during the demonstration brought sympathy from many French-worker unions, which called for a one-day general strike on May 13.

During the week beginning May 20, over ten million French workers went out on strike. Inspired by the student protests, the workers used the civil unrest as an opportunity to demand higher wages, better working conditions and the ousting of Charles de Gaulle as French president. De Gaulle responded by saying that France faced civil war and was "on the brink of paralysis". His words were followed by several hundred protesting students storming the Paris stock exchange and setting it alight. Within hours, the fire in the stock exchange had been put out and it emerged that de Gaulle had fled the country for Germany.

As the French government seemed close to collapse, Charles de Gaulle considered standing down. But after being assured that he still had control of the military, if not the country, de Gaulle decided to try to stay in power. Although the national television service was on strike, de Gaulle made an announcement on French radio that he would dissolve the country's national assembly so a snap election could take place on June 23. He also ordered all striking workers to return to work or he would institute a state of emergency. In the end, most strikers did return to work and the students called off their street demonstrations. As the movement lost its momentum many people came out in support of de Gaulle, who subsequently won the election on June 23.

❧

In the spring of 1968, Paris stunned the world with student and worker protests that nearly brought the country to its knees. The unrest began at the Sorbonne University's Nanterre campus, where students had been voicing their dissatisfaction for months over their underfunded education system. On May 2, the police shut down the university, which led to several days of marches, demonstrations and riots. The worst of the violence occurred on May 6, as police fired teargas and charged at crowds of over 20,000 marching students and university teachers with their batons raised. After several hours of clashes between protestors and the police, the city's cultural centre, St-Germain-des-Prés, resembled a battlefield.

Shop windows were smashed, bus tyres slashed and cars overturned, as Red Cross workers in helmets ducked under clouds of teargas to give first aid to hundreds of casualties. Television images of students covered with blood were broadcast to shocked audiences around the world, as police clubbed protestors armed with stones and torn-up pieces of tarmac. More riots followed on May 10, as worker and student unions called for a nationwide strike against "police repression" and demanded the release of all arrested protestors. On May 13, over one million students and striking workers marched through the streets of Paris.

The government tried to placate the protestors by announcing the release of the prisoners and the reopening of the Sorbonne. However, this did not prevent further protests, which culminated in the burning of the Paris stock exchange, President Charles de Gaulle fleeing the country and a nationwide strike of millions of French workers. In the end, however, the revolution did not come, although the Paris protests are considered a moral and cultural turning point in the country's modern history. They also inspired similar actions around the world, as students and workers demonstrated against the Vietnam War and their own authoritarian governments.

———∞∞∞∞———

A Timeline: the Before, During, and After of the Paris Student Protests

March 8, 1968 A Polish political crisis begins after University of Warsaw students are beaten with clubs during a march for student rights.

March 16, 1968 Over 400 University of Rome students are arrested after protesting against Italian police brutality.

March 16, 1968 An anti-Vietnam War protest outside the U.S. embassy in Grosvenor Square, London, leads to hours of street fighting between police and demonstrators.

April 1968 Students invade the Sorbonne University's Nanterre administration building.

May 2, 1968 The Sorbonne University is closed down by French authorities.

May 6, 1968 Paris student protests erupt into five hours of rioting with police.

May 7, 1968 A 50,000-strong march against police brutality turns into further violent clashes in Paris's Latin Quarter.

May 10, 1968 Another huge crowd congregates on Paris's Left Bank. Occupations and demonstrations soon spread throughout France.

May 13, 1968 Over a million people march through Paris as the police stay largely out of sight.

May 14, 1968 French workers begin occupying factories across the country.

May 18, 1968 Two million French workers are out on strike.

May 20, 1968 Striking worker numbers escalate to ten million – two-thirds of the French workforce.

May 30, 1968 Nearly 500,000 protestors march through Paris.

June 6, 1968 The French crisis comes to an end.

June 23, 1968 Charles de Gaulle wins the snap election.

August 1968 Russian troops invade Czechoslovakia to put an end to a four-month period of freedom known as the Prague Spring.

October 1968 Police, paratroopers and paramilitary units fire on protesting students in Mexico City.

NELSON MANDELA RELEASED FROM PRISON

1990

"If you want to make peace with your enemy, you have to work with your enemy. Then he becomes your partner."

Nelson Mandela speaks about reconciliation after being freed from prison.

Mandela was born in 1918, in South Africa's Transkei, to a chieftain of the Tembu people. Mandela's childhood was split between his tribal roots and a growing desire for a modern English life. He was given the tribal forename "Rolihlahla", a Xhosa term that means "troublemaker", but he was commonly known as Nelson, a name given to him by his teacher. Rejecting his family's wishes for an arranged marriage, Mandela went to Johannesburg and graduated with a law degree in 1942. His political activism began in 1943, when he marched for a bus boycott to reverse a bus-fair rise. Mandela then joined the ANC and co-founded its Youth League in 1944. In 1953, Mandela and long-time friend and collaborator, Oliver Tambo, set up South Africa's first black law firm, which offered legal advice to black people.

From 1952, Mandela advocated similar methods of civil disobedience used by Gandhi against British rule in India, including strikes and street marches. Thousands gathered to hear Mandela speak about his campaign against the government, including during a rally in Durban that saw Mandela briefly imprisoned. As Mandela's protests grew so did the ANC membership, which increased from 20,000 to 100,000 within a matter of months. In response, the government ordered mass arrests and introduced martial law through the Public Safety Act of 1953. By 1956, Mandela considered revising his non-violent methods to include a more direct militant approach. This he put into practice following the Sharpeville Massacre of 1960, which also led to his arrest in 1964 and imprisonment for 27 years.

In 1989, F.W. de Klerk became the president of South Africa and called for the abandonment of apartheid. He lifted the government's previous ban on protest marches and abolished elements of apartheid such as segregated public spaces. When de Klerk released ANC leader Walter Sisulu in 1989, it looked as though change was to become a reality. This was confirmed on February 11, 1990, when Nelson Mandela was released from prison. On May 4, while violence in black homelands raged in the background, Mandela met with de Klerk to discuss how to bring about stability.

On April 27, 1994, millions of black South Africans took up their right to vote for the first time in the country's first democratic general election. Nelson Mandela won by a landslide margin to become South Africa's first black president. Known in South Africa as 'the founding father of democracy', Mandela stood down from the presidency in 1999. One of the most recognizable figures in the world, Mandela continued to use his fame to promote good causes, including raising awareness of the deadly HIV/AIDS virus. He died on December 5, 2013 at the age of 95, leading to widespread mourning.

When Nelson Mandela was released from his 27-year imprisonment, he did not seek revenge or retribution against his white oppressors, but reconciliation. In 1964, Mandela had been sentenced for treason against the state and narrowly avoided the death penalty. By incarcerating the leader of the African National Congress (ANC), the government of South Africa thought it could silence opposition to its apartheid rule. Instead, Mandela became a symbol for the fight against apartheid, which led to his eventual release and the abandonment of the apartheid system. Apartheid, or "apart-hood", was introduced in 1948 by the National Party and relegated black South Africans to lives of servitude.

Mandela began his struggle against it when he joined the ANC as a law student in Johannesburg and helped found its youth league Although advocating a policy of non-violent protests, Mandela was repeatedly arrested for seditious activities, which led to his unsuccessful prosecution in the Treason Trial of 1956. However, Mandela put aside civil disobedience following the 1960 Sharpeville Massacre, which left 69 protestors dead when they were fired on by police. The government declared a state of emergency and banned the ANC. In response, Mandela sought out military support for the party in other countries. On his return, he was arrested and imprisoned.

Over the next 27 years, international pressure, boycotts and economic sanctions helped to force the government into freeing him. Mandela's release would see the end of apartheid, the first multiracial elections in South Africa and his swearing in as president. After 300 years of white rule, Mandela's inauguration speech did not urge wrath or rancour, but truth, reconciliation and the unification of black and white South Africans. At the time of his death, Mandela was a symbol for democracy, freedom, human rights and the fight against oppression.

———◦◦◇◦◦———

A Timeline: the Life, Experience and Influence of Nelson Mandela

1918 Rolihlahla (later Nelson) Mandela is born at Mvezo in South Africa's Transkei.

1939 Mandela enrols at the University College of Fort Hare.

1941 Mandela escapes an arranged marriage and begins working at the law firm Witkin, Sidelsky and Eidelman.

1944 Mandela co-founds the ANC Youth League (ANCYL) and marries Evelyn Ntoko Mase.

1952 Mandela is elected president of the ANCYL.

1952 As the campaign of defiance begins, Mandela is arrested and charged for violating the Suppression of Communism Act. Mandela is sentenced to nine months imprisonment with hard labor, suspended for two years.

1956 Mandela is arrested for treason along with 155 other members of the African National Congress. All are acquitted by March 29.

1958 Mandela divorces Evelyn Mase and marries Nomzamo "Winnie" Madikizela.

1960 The ANC is banned after the Sharpeville Massacre.

1961 Mandela forms the militant Umkhonto we Sizwe or "Spear of the Nation".

July 1962 Mandela leaves South Africa for military training and to garner support for the ANC.

November 1962 Mandela is sentenced to five years in prison for incitement and leaving the country without a passport.

1963 Mandela appears in court for the "Rivonia Trial" with other ANC leaders, including Walter Sisulu.

June 1964 Mandela arrives on Robben Island after being sentenced to life imprisonment for treason.

1985 Mandela rejects South Africa's then president P.W. Botha's offer to release him if he renounces violence.

February 2, 1990 The ban on the ANC is lifted.

February 11, 1990 Mandela is released from prison.

April 1994 Mandela is elected South Africa's first black president.

December 1994 Mandela publishes his autobiography, *Long Walk to Freedom*.

1999 Mandela steps down after one term as president and establishes the Nelson Mandela Foundation.

December 5, 2013 Mandela dies at home in Johannesburg aged 95.

CULTURE
AND SOCIETY

The Changing Face of Past Life: *T. Rex*

The Invention of the Model T Ford

Roald Amundsen Reaches the South Pole

The *Titanic* Sinks

The Wall Street Stock-Market Crash

Hillary Conquers Everest

The Beatles Release *Please Please Me*

THE CHANGING FACE OF PAST LIFE: *T. REX*

1902

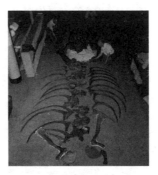

"Quarry No. 1 contains [several bones] of a large carnivorous dinosaur not described by Marsh...I have never seen anything like it from the Cretaceous."

Barnum Brown, in a letter to the American Natural History Museum describing his find in 1902.

People have been finding and digging up the fossilized bones of long-dead animals for centuries without knowing what they were. In China, they were often considered to be dragon bones. The first realization that fossils were the remains of prehistoric creatures came with the work of Georges Cuvier in Napoleon's France. In 1808, he identified a war trophy taken from Maastricht in Holland as the fossil of an extinct marine lizard, now called *Mososaurus*. The recognition that there had been former ages, with creatures now extinct, was revolutionary. In the following years, fossil hunters such as Mary Anning and Gideon Mantell uncovered evidence of large creatures that went by sea and by land.

In 1842, Richard Owen put the pieces together, establishing the new sub-order (now clade) *Dinosauria* to hold these "fearfully great reptiles". The suggestion that there had been an age long before humans when the Earth was ruled by giant, egg-laying lizards was a challenge to the Christian view that God had created all creatures in an unchanging world 6,000 years previously.

The second half of the 19th century was the age of the great dinosaur hunters. Othniel Marsh and Edward Cope competed to find the most and biggest dinosaurs, uncovering *Stegosaurus*, *Triceratops*, *Allosaurus* and *Diplodocus* between the 1870s and 1900. Cope alone named 1,200 species of dinosaur.

Then in 1909 came another revolutionary discovery: a vast field of fossils, far older than those of the dinosaurs. At Burgess Shale in Canada, Charles Walcott discovered soft-bodied animals and plants fossilized in great numbers. He returned year after year, amassing over 65,000 fossils, but their full importance was not recognized until the 1960s. The fossils of the Burgess Shale date from the Cambrian explosion, the sudden and rapid diversification of life around 542 million years ago. The fossils are also now studied by climatologists trying to project the effect of warming on Earth.

Marrying the fossil record with the way evolution was thought to progress was a challenge. That was accomplished in the 1930s and 1940s by several biologists, geneticists and palaeontologists. The modern evolutionary synthesis developed in the 1940s remains, in essence, the main paradigm in evolutionary theory. It shows evolution to be gradual, not directed towards any goal or perfection, and with many unsuccessful organisms failing along the way. It also demonstrates how the microevolution of genetics can produce the macroevolution seen in the fossil record.

In 1900, the first hints of a thrilling monster from the past surfaced in Wyoming, U.S.A. The eccentric palaeontologist Barnum Brown uncovered part of the skull and jaw, and some formidable teeth, from a dinosaur he named *Dynamosaurus imperiosus*. Two years later, in 1902, he found a complete skeleton. Not recognizing it as the same creature, he called the new, terrifyingly large carnivore *Tyrannosaurus rex*. It's difficult to imagine now how the discovery of *T. rex* must have changed the perception of dinosaurs, previously known mostly through the fish-eating plesiosaurs and huge land-going plant-eaters.

Barnum Brown, named after a circus strongman, was something of a real-life Indiana Jones. He attended digs in a full-length beaver-fur coat and a top hat, used dynamite to blast apart hillsides and did a great deal to popularize dinosaurs. He was also a spy. He was one of the greatest dinosaur hunters, finding so many fossils that there are still unopened crates of his finds awaiting investigation.

T. rex has become the public ambassador of the dinosaurs, more familiar than many living creatures. The iconic killing machine has captivated generations and ensured continuing investment in dinosaur palaeontology.

T. rex is the only dinosaur that is commonly known to the public by its full scientific name, described by American palaeontologist Robert T. Baker as "just irresistible to the tongue."

A Timeline: the Before, During, and After of the Discovery of the *T. Rex*

1677 Robert Plot includes the first illustration of a dinosaur bone in a book, *The Natural History of Oxfordshire*. He believed it to be a thigh bone from a giant human.

1808 French naturalist Georges Cuvier describes a giant marine lizard from a fossil found in Maastricht, Holland, and seized by Napoleon's army as a war trophy.

1809 William Smith finds an *Iguanodon* shin bone, but it was not recognized as such until the 1970s.

1811 Mary Anning finds a large ichthyosaur fossil at Lyme Regis, England.

1824 William Buckland names *Megalosaurus* from a jawbone that had been in Oxford's university museum since 1818; this was the first named dinosaur.

1825 Gideon Mantell describes *Iguanodon*.

1877 Benjamin Franklin Mudge and Samuel Wendell Williston find the first *Diplodocus* fossil, named the following year by Othniel Marsh.

1909 Charles Walcott discovers pre-Cambrian fossils at Burgess Shale, British Columbia.

1944 George Gaylord Simpson outlines modern evolutionary synthesis, bringing evolution, palaeontology and genetics together.

1964 After discovering *Deinonychus*, John Ostrum suggests that birds are the descendants of dinosaurs and might have been warm-blooded, sparking the "dinosaur renaissance" of the 1970s.

1978 A giant crater is found on the seabed at Chicxulub, Mexico.

1982 It is discovered that five mass extinctions have occurred in Earth's past.

1991 Alan Hildebrand and others suggest that the Chicxulub crater was left by an asteroid or comet that caused the mass extinction that killed the non-avian dinosaurs.

THE INVENTION OF THE MODEL T FORD

JULY 30, 1863–APRIL 7, 1947

"If everyone is moving forward together,
then success takes care of itself."

Henry Ford explains his theory for a prosperous society.

Henry Ford's car-making career began after building the "Quadricycle" in his shed and basement. He drove his first-ever automobile through the streets of Detroit in 1896, and the Quadricycle attracted enough interest from financial backers to enable Ford to form the Detroit Automobile Company in 1899. The company was dissolved in 1901, however, after Ford refused to deliver automobiles he considered of a low quality. Ford similarly left the Henry Ford Motor Company bearing his name after a dispute in 1902. He went on to form his famous Ford Motor Company in 1903.

Between 1903 and 1908, the Ford Motor Company manufactured the car models A, B, AC, F, R and S, followed by the highly successful Model N. But none matched the skyrocketing sales of the Model T, buyers of which had to be put on a waiting list so the order schedule could be fulfilled. An automobile affordable to middle-income workers, the Model T brought about rapid change to the American economy and the way people lived and worked. Farms became less isolated, the horse became a redundant form of transport, and cities spread outwards into the suburbs, creating a house-buying boom.

When his Highland Park factory opened in 1913, it featured the first moving automobile assembly line in the world. This advanced production technology meant a Model T Ford chassis could be turned out every 93 minutes instead of 728 minutes as before. Ford then announced he would pay his employees a $5-a-day wage for an eight-hour work day, rather than the previous $2.34 for a nine-hour day. The improved wage was twice what automobile workers were paid elsewhere and made Ford famous around the world. Branded as a humanist and socialist, Ford said he was able to pay his workers more because of the efficiency of production. By giving his workers a living wage and offering them reasonably priced goods, Ford made his employees consumers. This concept became known as "Fordism".

After purchasing a newspaper called the *Dearborn Independent* in 1919, Ford began publishing anti-Semitic articles under the headline "The International Jew: The World's Problem". Ford's attacks blamed Jews for provoking violence and financing war. His views won him adulation in Nazi Germany: Adolf Hitler, in particular, was a great admirer of Ford and kept a photo of him in his office. After a libel suit was brought against Ford by Jewish farm co-operative organizer Aaron Sapiro, he was forced to retract his remarks, issue an apology and shut down the newspaper. Ford was later said to have suffered a stroke after seeing newsreel footage taken during the liberation of Nazi concentration camps.

When the first Model T Ford rolled off the assembly line in 1908, Henry Ford fulfilled his promise to "democratize the automobile". Up until then, the car was a luxury item built by a team of mechanics that only the rich could afford to buy. But Ford's Model T, popularly known as the "Tin Lizzie", changed all that.

To cut costs, the Model T was constructed along an assembly line instead of in a workshop. This enabled a team of workers to perform a specific task on the machine as it traveled down the assembly line trackway. Assembly-line production slashed the price of a Model T from $850 to $300, making it the affordable "motorcar for the multitudes" that Ford had aspired to produce. The Model T became instantly popular, so much so that the Ford factories could not fulfil the millions of orders that poured in.

Between 1909 and 1927, Ford sold 15 million Model Ts and opened factories in England, France and Germany to keep up with demand. In the United States, Model T sales comprised up to 40 percent of the market share, even despite criticisms that the car itself was "no beauty". Produced mainly in black, the Model T had a four-cylinder, water-cooled engine, two forward gears, one reverse gear and a top speed of 72kph (45mph). The Model T and assembly-line production transformed economies and societies around the world as automobile industries flourished. Tourism became a major industry and gas stations, highways, motels and camp grounds sprang up everywhere as consumers hit the road.

A period of urbanization followed as families moved away from rural areas and into new city suburbs. The Model T was prized for its low cost and durability, but it also profoundly changed the way Americans lived, worked and traveled in the 20th century. It also introduced mass consumerism to modern society.

—◦◦×◦◦—

A Timeline: the Life, Experience and Influence of Henry Ford

1879 Henry Ford leaves his family farm to move to Detroit and pursue a career in machinery.

1886 The first modern automobile, the Benz Patent-Motorwagen, is built by German inventor Carl Benz.

1893 The Duryea brothers build the first American petrol-powered car.

1896 Ford shows his first automobile, the "Quadricycle", to the world.

1897 German Rudolf Diesel invents the first car powered by a diesel engine.

1901 Ford enters one of his cars in a race at the Detroit Driving Club, Grosse Pointe, Michigan, and wins. The victory brings him much attention from financial backers.

1902 Ransom E. Olds begins the mass production of U.S. cars at his Oldsmobile factory.

1903 In a partnership with Detroit coal dealer Alexander Malcomson, Ford forms the Ford Motor Company with $28,000 in cash and $21,000 from private investors.

1910 The Cadillac Motor Company introduces electric key ignition.

1914 The Ford factory at Highland Park receives 10,000 job applications after a $5-a-day wage is announced for Ford employees.

1908 The Model T Ford, or "Tin Lizzie", is released.

1915 Ford announces he will travel on an ocean liner to Europe to try to convince warring leaders to declare peace. His plans end in failure.

1921 Citroën in France begins the assembly-line production of cars.

1927 Production begins at Ford's River Rouge factory, where all of the raw materials used to build automobiles are owned by Ford.

1929 Ford institutes a $7-a-day wage for his workers to try to stave off the effects of the Great Depression. It fails, and he is forced to lay off half of his workforce.

1940 All cars are now mass produced, but only 17 car makers of the 200 that began in 1920 have survived.

1947 Ford dies at the age of 83.

ROALD AMUNDSEN REACHES THE SOUTH POLE

JULY 16, 1872–JUNE 18, 1928

"The holiday humor that ought to have prevailed in the tent that evening – our first on the plateau – did not make its appearance: there was depression and sadness in the air; we had grown so fond of our dogs."

Roald Amundsen describes slaughtering the sled dogs for meat during his attempt on the South Pole

Although studying to become a doctor, on his mother's wishes, the 21-year-old Roald Amundsen quit university for the maritime life as soon as she died. After working on various ships that traveled to the Arctic, Amundsen became first mate on the *Belgica* – the first ship to spend a winter in Antarctica after it became trapped by pack ice in 1887. Amundsen learned valuable lessons from the voyage, including how to prevent scurvy by eating the meat of animals that produce vitamin C.

With a crew of six men aboard his 47-tonne ship the *Gjøa*, Amundsen began a mission to be the first to sail through the Northwest Passage – which connects the Atlantic and Pacific Oceans – and then around the northern Canadian coast. After traveling through the passage and reaching Cape Colborne in 1905, the *Gjøa* was halted by ice and spent the winter on Herschel Island. When the mission was concluded in 1906, Amundsen and his crew were given a heroes' welcome at their final destination of Nome, Alaska. The voyage inspired Amundsen to attempt more "firsts" and he prepared for a mission to reach the North Pole.

Amundsen's plan to sail to the Arctic aboard his new ship the *Fram* changed when he heard that American Robert Peary had reached the North Pole in 1909. Instead, Amundsen prepared the *Fram* to sail to the Antarctic, although he kept the mission a secret from virtually everyone he knew. Amundsen set sail in June 1910 and steered the *Fram* to the Bay of Whales, Antarctica. From the Bay of Whales, Amundsen was 97km (60 miles) closer to the South Pole than his rival Robert Falcon Scott, who also arrived in January 1911 for his attempt on the Pole. In the end, Scott would not reach the Pole until after Amundsen and the mission would then claim his life and those of his men. Amundsen, by contrast, returned home a victorious hero.

Following his Antarctic success, Amundsen bought a new ship, the *Maud*, and in 1918 prepared once again to sail to the North Pole. However, he had to abandon his plans and instead set about reaching the North Pole by airplane. In 1925, Amundsen and American explorer Lincoln Ellsworth traveled to within 242km (150 miles) of the Pole but did not succeed in passing over it. Then in 1926, Amundsen, Ellsworth and Italian engineer Umberto Nobile managed to fly over the North Pole in an airship. The three men were reported to have thrown their national flags from the airship as they passed over the Pole. Amundsen became embroiled in a dispute over credit for the North Pole flight in his later years, and he died while trying to rescue Nobile from an airship crash near Svalbard in 1928.

By the time Roald Amundsen reached the point where his rival Ernest Shackleton had given up and turned back, victory was close at hand. Aided by fair weather and dog-pulled sleds, Amundsen reached the South Pole on December 14, 1911, and hoisted the Norwegian flag.

The explorer, who as a child slept with his window open during winter to prepare for the Arctic cold, made sure each of his four men held the flag as it was planted. The mission had been a team effort, but it was the sled dogs that had seen them over the line. Amundsen knew the value of the dogs, describing them as "the most important thing for us. The whole outcome of the expedition depends on them."

However, of the 52 dogs that were hand-picked for the mission, only 16 of them saw the South Pole – the rest provided valuable meat for the journey there and back. Amundsen's decision to use dogs was in grave contrast to the failed Scott expedition that employed ponies and perished to a man after giving chase to the Norwegians. After naming his spot at the South Pole "Polheim", or "Pole Home", Amundsen's team turned around and began the long journey home.

By the time they reached their expedition base at the Bay of Whales on January 25, 1912, Amundsen's team had traveled for 99 days and covered 2,995km (1,860 miles). Amundsen returned from his adventure a national hero and he continued on other voyages of discovery afterwards. In the end, Amundsen would die in the same heroic manner as he had lived his life: he was killed in 1928 when his plane crashed into the Arctic Ocean during a rescue mission. Amundsen had spoken of his love for the Arctic only a few months earlier, saying, "If only you knew how splendid it is up there, that's where I want to die."

A Timeline: the Life, Experience and Influence of Roald Amundsen

1773 Captain James Cook and his crew become the first men to cross the Antarctic Circle.

1820 Russian Fabian Gottlieb von Bellingshausen becomes the first person to see the Antarctic continent.

1823 Englishman James Weddell sails to 74 degrees south – the southernmost point ever sailed. The Weddell Sea today bears his name.

1841 While searching for the South Magnetic Pole, James Clark Ross discovers the Ross Sea, Ross Island and the Ross Ice Shelf.

1892 Captain Carl Larsen lands on Seymour Island near the Antarctic peninsula.

1895 Henry Bull lands at Cape Adare and discovers lichen, the first sign of plant life in the Antarctic.

1898 Roald Amundsen and the crew of the *Belgica* become trapped in the pack ice off the Antarctic peninsula and become the first people to survive an Antarctic winter.

1899 Carsten Borchgrevink and the crew of the *Southern Cross* land at Cape Adare and become the first to spend the winter on Antarctic ground.

1902 Robert Falcon Scott, Edward Wilson and Ernest Shackleton attempt to reach the South Pole, but bad weather forces them to return home.

1906 Roald Amundsen completes his voyage through the Northwest Passage, making him the first person to do so.

1908 Ernest Shackleton, Eric Marshall, Frank Wild and Jameson Adams attempt to reach the South Pole, but have to abandon the attempt because of hunger and ill health.

1911 Roald Amundsen and his team of four men reach the South Pole and return unharmed.

1912 Robert Falcon Scott, Edward Wilson, Edgar Evans and Lawrence Oates reach the South Pole to find Amundsen has beaten them to it. All four die from hunger and cold on the return journey.

1915 Ernest Shackleton abandons his attempt to cross the Antarctic continent and, after a torturous journey, returns home in 1917. Just three men are missing from his crew.

1928 Amundsen dies trying to rescue his friend Umberto Nobile from an airship crash in the Arctic Ocean.

1957 As part of the International Geophysical Year, scientists from 67 countries visit Antarctica and 12 new bases are constructed.

1959 The 12 leading nations that participated in the International Geophysical Year sign the Antarctic Treaty, stating the continent "shall continue forever to be used exclusively for peaceful purposes".

THE *TITANIC* SINKS

1912

"Deeply regret advise you *Titanic* sank this morning after
collision with iceberg, resulting in serious loss of life.
Full particulars later."

White Star Line chairman Bruce Ismay in his telegraph to the White
Star Line after surviving the *Titanic* disaster and landing in New York.

In 1909 the keel was laid for *Titanic*, one of three Olympic-class ocean
liners commissioned by the White Star Line. Designed to outdo their
competitor in transatlantic sea travel – Cunard – White Star Line's new
ships promised greater levels of speed and luxury to their passengers.
The ships would also be the largest sea-going vessels in the world,
powered by three main engines and weighing around 46,000 tons. Over
600 tons of coal a day was needed to power *Titantic*'s engines, enabling
a top speed of 45kph (28mph). Called the "Millionaire's Special",
Titanic's maiden voyage included a range of prominent and wealthy
passengers, including American businessman Benjamin Guggenheim,
Macy's department-store owner Isidor Straus, White Star Line chairman
J. Bruce Ismay and the ship's designer Thomas Andrews.

Titanic's journey between Southampton and New York was a highly publicized event, proudly celebrated by all involved. However, the hubristic belief that she was unsinkable led to basic safety measures being overlooked. These included the low number of lifeboats on board the ship and the reports of icebergs in the area being ignored by some of the ship's crew.

A U.S. investigation led by Senator William Alden Smith found contributing factors to *Titanic's* sinking included the failure of Captain Smith to slow the ship after receiving iceberg warnings and regulatory failures over the lack of lifeboats on board. Passenger testimony also reported that the lifeboats were not launched at full capacity, and that the lack of a general warning meant that many passengers were not aware of the impending danger. The investigation's strongest criticism was meted out to the *Californian*, a ship that was less than 31km (19 miles) away from the sinking *Titanic* but ignored its distress signals. A later British enquiry blamed the excessive speed at which *Titanic* was traveling as the main cause for the collision. The *Titanic* disaster led to changes in maritime safety, and regulations that required all ships have enough lifeboat space for every passenger as well as a compulsory 24-hour radio watch.

Because of the lack of available technology at the time of *Titanic's* sinking, the first serious attempts to view the wreckage did not come until 1985. Then, a French–American expedition used a 5m (16ft) submersible called the *Argo* to take video footage of the wreck and send it to a live monitor above water. Traveling to a depth of 4,000m (13,120ft) at the bottom of the Atlantic Ocean, the *Argo* showed the ship lying upright in two pieces. The footage helped piece together the ship's last moments before it went under and inspired James Cameron's 1997 blockbuster movie, *Titanic*. The movie became the highest-grossing film in history and sparked a renewed round of public interest in the *Titanic* disaster.

Titanic was designed to be the last word in ocean travel: a luxurious colossus that could carry 3,547 passengers and was said to be unsinkable. Targeting the large numbers of emigrants and wealthy travelers crossing the Atlantic, *Titanic's* owners spared no expense fitting out its opulent interior. The ship was described as a floating palace, which featured four elevators, a lavish first-class saloon and a swimming pool. At 269m (882ft) long, *Titanic* was not only the largest but also the most technologically advanced ship in the world. The steamship's double-bottomed hull was divided into 16 compartments, each of which could be closed off if the hull was breached. The ship's architects boasted that even if four of the 16 compartments were flooded, *Titanic* would still stay afloat.

Their great error, however, was that the compartments were not capped at the top, leaving a gap for water to move through. In the end, *Titanic's* maiden voyage was not only destined to be her last: it would also result in the greatest peacetime maritime disaster of the 20th century. The tragedy began around 644km (400 miles) south of Newfoundland, when an iceberg was sighted in *Titanic's* path. Despite taking evasive action, the ship was traveling too fast to avoid a collision. At 11:40pm the hull on the starboard side of *Titanic* was breached and five of its 16 compartments filled with water. This, in turn, tipped the ship forwards and caused the remaining compartments to also fill with seawater. Two hours and 40 minutes later, *Titanic* sank.

With only enough lifeboats for 1,178 of the 2,223 passengers on board, many people perished in the freezing waters. The arrival of the Cunard liner *Carpathia* 80 minutes after the *Titanic* sank prevented a greater loss of life, but in the end the death toll stood at over 1,500. Intrigue about the passengers' last hours aboard their glamorous and ill-fated vessel continues today in articles, books, television programs and films.

A Timeline: the Before, During, and After of the *Titanic*

1850 The White Star Line is founded.

1898 *Futility* is published, a fictional book about a British liner named *Titan* that sinks after hitting an iceberg on her maiden voyage across the Atlantic Ocean, resulting in great loss of life.

1907 The idea to build *Titanic* and its Olympic-class sister ships, *Olympic* and *Britannic*, is conceived over dinner between White Star Line chairman J. Bruce Ismay and shipbuilder William James Pirrie.

1911 *Titanic*'s hull is successfully launched before a crowd of 10,000 spectators.

April 10 1912 At 12 noon, *Titanic* sets sail from Southampton for New York. Four days later she sinks.

April 18 1912 The *Carpathia*, carrying *Titanic* survivors, lands in New York to a press frenzy. It takes four days for a full list of the dead to be posted.

April/May 1912 The White Star Line commissions four Canadian ships to recover the bodies of the dead from the sea. Only 333 bodies in total are found.

May 1912 Insurers Lloyds of London pay the White Star Line £1,000,000 for the disaster. Charities are then set up to provide financial support to those who lost family members, one continuing into the 1960s.

May 1912 *Saved from the Titanic*, the first film about the *Titanic* starring actual survivor Dorothy Gibson, is released. Gibson suffers a nervous breakdown after making the film.

July 1912 An investigation into the sinking of *Titanic* blames the tragedy on excessive speed, lack of lifeboats and the breakdown of communication regarding icebergs.

1913 An international Ice Patrol is set up to warn ships of iceberg activity in shipping lanes. No ships since *Titanic* have been lost to an iceberg in the patrol area.

1914 The International Convention for the Safety of Life at Sea is formed to ensure safety standards aboard seagoing vessels.

1955 The first book about *Titanic*, *A Night to Remember*, is published.

1985 The wreckage of *Titanic* is explored by submersible the *Argo*.

1997 Winner of 11 Academy Awards, James Cameron's *Titanic* movie starring Kate Winslet and Leonardo DiCaprio is released.

2009 Millvina Dean, the last living survivor of *Titanic*, dies. Just nine weeks old at the time of the disaster, Dean was the youngest passenger on board.

2012 Plans are announced by Australian businessman Clive Palmer to build a *Titanic* replica, named *Titanic II*.

2012 The Titanic Belfast, a museum and memorial center to *Titanic*, opens by the shipyards where it was built.

THE WALL STREET STOCK-MARKET CRASH

1929

"So, first of all, let me assert my firm belief that the only thing we have to fear is fear itself."

President Franklin D. Roosevelt tries to console the American public during his inauguration speech.

After the panic selling on Black Thursday, Wall Street financiers tried to stabilize the market by buying up as many shares as they could. This offered a temporary lull, but by Black Tuesday an even greater sense of panic swept the stock-exchange floor. One eyewitness account reported that brokers "hollered and screamed, they clawed at one another's collars. It was like a bunch of crazy men." Others collapsed where they stood as the value of shares fell through the floor and selling orders made it impossible for the Exchange to keep up with the transactions. By the end of the day more than 30 billion dollars had been lost – more than twice the national debt.

Following the calamitous events of the 1929 stock-market crash, the Great Depression began. The effects were felt across the world but nowhere as keenly as in North America, where millions lost their jobs, savings and then homes, as they became unable to pay their mortgages. By 1932, the number of homeless people reached more than two million and many were forced to live in large cardboard shantytowns, mockingly called "Hoovervilles" after the much-maligned president. The food served on the many soup lines was similarly referred to as "Hoover Stew".

Despite introducing measures such as the Hoover Dam project to stimulate the economy, President Hoover was heavily defeated by his opponent Franklin D. Roosevelt in the general election of 1932. Roosevelt swept into power on the basis of his "New Deal" manifesto, which promised change according to the "Three Rs": Relief, Recovery, and Reform. Under the New Deal, Roosevelt spent over $6 billion on public works to create jobs and revive the economy. He also tried to endear the American public to politicians once more through his evening "fireside chats" on the radio.

From 1934 to 1940, a severe drought hit many of the states of the American Great Plains, destroying crops and bringing devastation to entire farming communities. Without plants to anchor the topsoil, wind storms buried a vast region in earth and dust, which then became known as the "Dust Bowl". Thousands of families from Kansas, Oklahoma, Texas, New Mexico and Colorado were forced to pack up their homes and travel to California to find seasonal work as a result of the Dust Bowl.

The 1920s was boom time in America. As the economy went from strength to strength, millions of Americans invested in the stock market. Even those of meagre means tried to get rich quick by playing the stock market on margin. This meant borrowing money to pay for shares and then using them as collateral against the loan. But at the end of the decade the good times came to a sudden, shuddering halt, as boom turned to bust.

On October 4, 1929, the market took a sharp dip and continued to slide throughout the month. October 21 saw an avalanche of selling, as many Americans tried to salvage something from their weakened portfolios. On October 24 – "Black Thursday" – panic swept the Wall Street stock exchange and investors ordered brokers to sell at any price. Worse was to come on October 29, known to history as "Black Tuesday" – the day Wall Street crashed. As the trading day ended, vast fortunes were lost and millions of ordinary Americans found themselves instantly bankrupt.

The stock-market crash then turned into the Great Depression, as millions of Americans lost their jobs, hundreds of banks closed and former millionaires took to selling apples on street corners. Mass misery ensued: some figures reported that over 23,000 people committed suicide in 1929 alone. President Herbert Hoover, however, refused to accept that the Great Depression would last. He proposed tax cuts and asked businesses to slash worker wages. Mass layoffs and unemployment followed: by 1933, 25 percent of American workers were without work. Hoover's response to the rising unemployment was to encourage private charities to offer help on the ground, as millions of people lost their homes and were forced to join soup kitchens. Hoover's failure to save America's economy led to the election of Democrat Franklin D. Roosevelt, who launched the "New Deal" and turned America into a social welfare state. Many nations around the world followed Roosevelt's example.

A Timeline: the Before, During, and After of the Wall Street Stock-market Crash

October 1929 After six years of prosperity, the Wall Street stock market crashes on October 29. As prices plummet, banks call in all loans, leading to the Great Depression.

1930 The knock-on effect of the Wall Street crash leads to a sharp decline in international trade, contributing to the worst global depression of the 20th century.

March–November 1930 Over 1.6 million people have become unemployed since the crash and the city streets of New York are crowded with thousands of unemployed people selling apples for five cents apiece.

1930 A severe drought starts in the Great Plains area, ruining millions of farms and leading to the Dust Bowl.

1931 Great Britain, Japan and the countries of Scandinavia leave the gold standard, the monetary system whereby a country's currency has a value linked to gold. There are banking crises in Austria and Germany.

February 1931 Food riots break out across the United States and looters make smash-and-grab attacks on grocery stores.

1931 New York's Bank of the United States collapses.

July 1932 The U.S. Reconstruction Finance Corporation is ordered to give money to struggling American states.

1932 Workers in London and other major cities protest over jobs cuts and worsening employment conditions. With public dissatisfaction at an all-time high, extremist groups such as the Nazi Party begin to gain support.

November 1932 Franklin D. Roosevelt is elected president in a landslide victory after receiving 22.8 million votes to Herbert Hoover's 15.75 million.

March 1933 Franklin D. Roosevelt delivers the first of his radio "fireside chats", during which he appeals to the nation to join him in "banishing fear".

April 1933 President Roosevelt takes the nation off the gold standard under the Emergency Banking Act.

August 1933 The government establishes the Soil Erosion Service in an attempt to address the years of drought blighting the farms of the Great Plains.

May 1934 A three-day dust storm blows topsoil as far east as New York and Boston, where street lights are lit during the day to enable people to see.

April 1935 President Roosevelt creates the Works Progress Administration, which employs over 8.5 million people to build roads, bridges and airports.

October 1936 The *San Francisco News* publishes a series of John Steinbeck articles about the Dust Bowl migrant camps. The articles will later inform his novel, *The Grapes of Wrath*.

November 1940 Franklin D. Roosevelt is elected to an unprecedented third term as president.

1941 The entry of America into the Second World War after the Japanese bombing of Pearl Harbor greatly improves the U.S. economy, as industries create jobs to support the war effort.

HILLARY CONQUERS EVEREST

1953

"Well, George, we knocked the bastard off."

Edmund Hillary's first words to his climbing companion and
lifelong friend George Lowe after conquering Everest.

At 16 years old, Edmund Hillary was a gangly and uncoordinated
teenager who spent his spare time reading books. But on a class
trip to Mount Ruapehu in New Zealand's North Island, Hillary
discovered a love for climbing. As an adult he took up an occupation
as a beekeeper, which allowed him to climb New Zealand's mountain
ranges during the winter. In 1948, Hillary made a successful ascent
of Aoraki, also known as Mount Cook, which is New Zealand's highest
peak at 3,754m (12,313ft) above sea level.

In 1951, a British expedition traveled to Everest to establish a route up the mountain via its southern face. The expedition members, which included Eric Shipton, Tom Bourdillon and Edmund Hillary, surveyed the mountain's Western Cym valley and concluded it would be possible to traverse through it and then on to the South Col. From the South Col an attempt on the summit could be mounted. The climbers spent the next month attempting to reach the Western Cwm through the Khumbu Icefall, but were defeated at the last hurdle – an impassable, 30m (98ft) wide crevasse.

News reached London on June 2,1953 that Hillary and Tenzing Norgay (often know as Sherpa Tenzing) of the British Everest Expedition had conquered the mountain. The *Times* reporter James Morris had sent the news from Mount Everest in a coded message that was taken to the village of Namche Bazaar in Nepal by a runner. The message was then relayed to London via a wireless transmitter. By the time Hillary returned to Kathmandu a few days later, it was to the news that he had been knighted. Intense media interest followed and everyone wanted to know who had stepped foot on the summit first. Tenzing later said that it had been Hillary.

Over the years following Hillary and Tenzing's conquest of Everest, dozens of people from different countries were able to emulate their accomplishment. Notable firsts included the first person to reach the summit without oxygen, the first woman to reach the top and the first person to climb Everest solo. However, amidst criticism that climbing the mountain had become too commercial, came one of the most lethal years in Everest's history. In May 1996, eight people died trying to reach the top of Everest when they were caught in a blizzard. Four more died later that year, also trying to reach the summit. Everest would claim 16 further victims during an avalanche in 2014, and another 19 died in 2015, during an avalanche caused by the Nepal earthquakes of that year.

As Edmund Hillary and Tenzing Norgay set foot on the summit of Everest, they gave each other a polite handshake – and then a joyful embrace. The New Zealand climber and his Nepalese Sherpa guide had just achieved what no other man had before: the ascent of the 8,848-m (29,021-ft) high Mount Everest, the highest point on the planet. Hillary and Tenzing had set out ten weeks earlier as part of the 1953 British Everest Expedition led by Colonel John Hunt.

The expedition, which included 362 porters, 20 Sherpa guides, a *Times* reporter and five tons of supplies, trekked for 274km (170 miles) from Kathmandu, Nepal, to the village of Namche Bazaar, which they reached on March 10. After three days of training, the expedition made its way to Mount Everest's base camp and then worked its way up the mountain's South Col. After the climbers pitched a base camp at 7,890m (25,879ft), Tom Bourdillon and Charles Evans made an attempt on the summit. The pair came within 91m (298ft) of the top, but had to turn back when Evans' oxygen system failed.

Hunt then ordered Hillary and Tenzing to try for the top. The climbers set out on May 26 and pitched a last tent 8,500m (27,880ft) above sea level. In the morning, Hillary's boots were frozen solid, and he had to warm them up before the final ascent. The last hurdle between the climbers and the top was a 12m (39ft) rock face, now known as the "Hillary Step". Hillary negotiated the cliff by inching himself up a crack in the rock and then hauling Tenzing up behind him. After reaching the summit at 11:30am on May 29, the pair took photographs, planted the flags of Britain, Nepal, the United Nations and India, and Norgay buried some sweets in the snow as a Buddhist offering. After 15 minutes, with their oxygen supply running low, the climbers began their descent back down the mountain.

A Timeline: the Life, Experience and Influence of Edmund Hillary

1922 The first attempt to reach the summit of Mount Everest fails, although members of the British expedition become the first humans to climb above 8,000m (26,240ft).

1924 British climbers George Mallory and Andrew Irvine are seen for the last time during their Everest ascent. Mallory's body was found in 1999.

1933 A British expedition to Everest's summit fails and climber Percy Wyn-Harris declares it "unclimbable".

1934 British eccentric Maurice Wilson dies during an attempt on Everest.

1935 Tenzing Norgay makes his first visit to Everest, as a porter employed for a British reconnaissance mission.

1938 Explorer Bill Tilman reaches 8,290m (27,191ft) without supplemental oxygen for the first time.

1947 Canadian Earl Denman enters Tibet illegally and is then defeated in his attempt on Everest.

1950 Nepal opens its borders to foreigners, making the easier southern route up the mountain accessible.

1951 British climbers including Eric Shipton, Edmund Hillary and Tom Bourdillon survey Everest's southern face.

1952 A Swiss expedition becomes the first to reach the Western Cwm.

1952 Edmund Hillary and climbing companion George Lowe fail in their attempt on Cho Oyu – Tibet's sixth-highest mountain.

1953 Edmund Hillary and Tenzing Norgay become the first people to reach the summit of Mount Everest.

1956 Four climbers from a Swiss expedition become the first people after Hillary to reach the top of Everest.

1970 Japanese climber Yuichiro Miura skis down Everest's South Col.

1975 Japanese climber Junko Tabei becomes the first woman to reach the top of Everest.

1975 A British expedition led by Chris Bonington achieves the first ascent of Everest via the Southwest Face.

1980 Italian Reinhold Messner becomes the first person to climb Everest solo and without an oxygen tank.

1988 Jean-Marc Boivin of France makes the first paraglider descent of Everest.

1990 Edmund Hillary's son becomes the first child of a summiter to reach the top of Everest.

2008 Edmund Hillary dies after dedicating his life to the Sherpa people of Nepal through his Himalayan Trust.

THE BEATLES RELEASE
PLEASE PLEASE ME

1963

"We sang it and George Martin said,
"Can we change the tempo?" We said, "What's that?"
He said, "Make it a bit faster. Let me try it."
And he did. We thought, "Oh, that's all right, yes.""

Paul McCartney describes the making of *Please Please Me*

In 1957, 16-year-old John Lennon formed a skiffle group called the Quarrymen with some friends from Liverpool's Quarry Bank School. Soon afterwards, Paul McCartney joined as guitarist, followed by George Harrison. After adding drummer Pete Best, the band played "beat music" in nightclubs around Liverpool. In 1960 they moved to Hamburg, Germany, where they often played in late-night clubs frequented by sailors. In late 1961, they moved back to Liverpool to take a spot at The Cavern Club. In 1961, a Liverpool record-store owner called Brian Epstein saw the Beatles perform at The Cavern Club and immediately asked the band to let him manage them.

Epstein sent British music labels the band's tape in the hope that someone would sign them. Epstein eventually managed to secure a deal with Parlophone, a subsidiary of EMI. The producer at Parlophone who took the Beatles under his wing was the classically trained musician, George Martin. Martin suggested they replace drummer Pete Best with the more professional Ringo Starr and rearrange *Please Please Me* from a slow lament into an uplifting pop romp. History was made.

After Beatlemania had gripped pop fans on both sides of the Atlantic – provoking the so-called British Invasion and dozens of moptop imitators – the Beatles announced their retirement from playing live. Instead, the band concentrated their efforts on recording and set to work developing an entirely different record to follow up the success of their 1966 *Revolver*. The result was the iconic 1967 *Sgt. Pepper's Lonely Hearts Club Band*, a revolutionary record that became the soundtrack for a new counterculture era of hedonism and uninhibited experimentation. Mind-expanding drugs, pacifism, free love and transcendental meditation were some of the themes that followed, as the hippie movement reached full bloom in the late 1960s.

However, at this time, personal disagreements began to break out among the Beatles' members, particularly between Paul McCartney and John Lennon, the band's leading songwriters. The Beatles had attempted to create their own company, Apple, but this had been badly mismanaged and the hard realities of financial management put a further stress on already-strained relationships. After their last studio album, *Abbey Road*, the Beatles split up in 1970. They later released *Let It Be*, an album of leftover songs. In the following years, all of the Beatles produced solo albums: John Lennon with his wife Yoko Ono and Paul McCartney with his wife Linda in his new outfit Wings. John Lennon was assassinated by a gunman in 1980, forever quashing the possibility of a Beatles reunion.

After having some moderate success with "Love Me Do", the Beatles kept their fingers crossed for the release of their next single, "Please Please Me". However, no one could have predicted what came next. "Please Please Me" turned out to be the groundbreaker that catapulted the Beatles to fame: it brought about the phenomenon called "Beatlemania", kicked off the "British Invasion" of America and introduced the world to the swinging sixties.

After "Please Please Me" went to number one in the UK charts, Beatles' producer George Martin was quick to get the band into the studio to cut their first album. Also called *Please Please Me*, the album was recorded in one 13-hour session, cost £400 to make and included eight original numbers from its 14-song playlist. A band playing so many of its own songs was a game-changer at a time when the charts were dominated by film soundtracks and easy-listening singers who had their music written for them.

The Beatles created a musical revolution for the throngs of screaming fans at the forefront of Beatlemania, but the band were far from newcomers to the scene. Cutting their teeth on Hamburg's "beat music" nightclubs and then taking up a residence at The Cavern Club in Liverpool, the Beatles were already a tight live band by the time their songs hit the charts. However, it was only through the pairing of producer George Martin and manager Brian Epstein that the "Fab Four" hit superstardom. Epstein told the band to drop their "teddy boy" image of leather jackets and coiffed hair and replace it with smart suits and moptop haircuts. This new, improved image, combined with the catchy musical style expertly recorded by master producer George Martin, was a formula that couldn't fail. The listening public could not get enough of *Please Please Me*: it stayed at number one for 30 weeks and was only replaced by the band's second album, *With the Beatles*.

A Timeline: the Life and Experience of the Beatles

—————◆•◆—————

1957 John Lennon and Paul McCartney's band the Quarrymen perform at The Cavern Club in Liverpool for the first time.

1960 The Quarrymen change their name to the Silver Beetles.

August 1960 The Silver Beetles change their name to the Beatles and play at the Indra Club in Hamburg for the first time.

December 1960 The band play their first British concert as the Beatles at the Casbah Coffee Club in Liverpool.

June 1962 The Beatles begin their first recording session at EMI with George Martin as producer.

October 1962 The Beatles first single, "Love Me Do", reaches number 17 in the charts.

January 1963 "Please Please Me" reaches number one in four of the five British singles charts. Twelve number-one hits follow.

November 1963 *With the Beatles* becomes the first million-selling album in Britain.

February 1964 The Beatles tour America for the first time and break television-viewing records on the *Ed Sullivan Show*.

July 1964 The Beatles' debut film, *A Hard Day's Night*, premieres.

October 1965 Queen Elizabeth II awards the four Beatles MBEs (Member of the British Empire). Lennon returns his MBE in 1969.

December 1965 December 1965 The more experimental album *Rubber Soul* is released.

April 1967 Beatles' manager Brian Epstein is found dead from a drug overdose.

June 1967 *Sgt. Pepper's Lonely Hearts Club Band* is released and stays at number one in Britain for 27 weeks.

January 1968 The Beatles' Apple company opens offices in London.

February 1968 The Beatles fly to India to meditate with the Maharishi Mahesh Yogi. Divisions appear among the band members for the first time.

January 1969 A documentary, *Let It Be*, is made that records great disharmony within the group.

1969 *Abbey Road* is recorded, with 20 August marking the last day all four Beatles are in a studio together.

April 1970 The Beatles officially break up.

TECHNOLOGY

The Wright Brothers' First Flight

The Discovery of Cosmic Radio Waves

John Logie Baird Shows TV to the World

Turing: Towards Thinking Machines

Altair 8800: the Dawn of Personal Computing

The World Wide Web

THE WRIGHT BROTHERS' FIRST FLIGHT

1903

"By original scientific research, the Wright brothers discovered the principles of human flight. As inventors, builders and flyers, they further developed the airplane, taught man to fly, and opened the era of aviation."

A plaque adorning the Wright brothers' Flyer at the Smithsonian.

Orville and Wilbur began funding their experimentation into flight by opening a bicycle-repair shop in Ohio in 1896. Spurred on by the gliding attempts of Germany's Otto Lilienthal, the brothers decided that pilot control was paramount to successful flying and that this could be achieved by powering a plane with an engine. The brothers also investigated wing shapes and created "wing warping", a method of twisting a wing to aid lateral control in the air. Wing warping was a precursor to the ailerons used today in modern aviation, which prevent an aircraft from rolling. With its soft sand and regular winds, the remote Kitty Hawk became the Wright brothers' regular testing ground for their glider flights.

The Wright brothers began trialling manned and unmanned gliders in 1900, using the biplane model favored in Europe. Despite flying for up to 122m (400ft), the brothers struggled with turning their craft and attaining lift while in flight. To remedy these problems, the brothers conducted more theoretical tests with miniature wings and a specially constructed wind tunnel. As a result, the brothers designed a longer, narrower wing that had an enhanced lift-to-drag ratio and is similar to the modern aircraft wings used today.

Following the success of their first flight in 1903, the Wright brothers went on to achieve a 38-minute flight in 1905 that covered 40km (24.5 miles). The press, however, did not attend the flight and remained unconvinced of the brothers' "alleged accomplishments". This was amplified in Paris, where an article on the brothers was headlined "FLYERS OR LIARS?". The brothers added to the controversy by refusing to make any further flight demonstrations until they had been offered a contract to produce planes for a commercial company or the military. In 1908, contracts with the U.S. military and a French syndicate rested on the brothers' ability to provide a successful demonstration of their Flyers. Orville's series of flying demonstrations in Le Mans, France, and Wilbur's demonstrations in Fort Myer, Virginia, made the brothers instant global celebrities.

The brothers' Wright Company became embroiled in a long patent lawsuit in 1909 over the use of ailerons by competing manufacturers. Despite tarnishing the brothers' public image, the lawsuit did not hinder the success of the Wright Company, which sold planes to the U.S. Army and also trained pilots. But the business and legal issues took their toll on Wilbur's health, and he died in 1912. In 1915, Orville sold his interest in the Wright Company and in 1917 the brothers' patent expired, signalling the end of legal issues for the company. Orville went on to work as an aircraft consultant and designed fighter planes during the First World War. He spent the last years of his life defending the Wright brothers' place as inventors of the airplane and died in 1948.

December 17, 1903 was a good day for flying in the sleepy fishing hamlet of Kitty Hawk, North Carolina. At 10:30am, Orville Wright climbed aboard his Flyer biplane as a steady headwind blew across the beach in front of him. Lying flat on the plane's wing section, Orville tested the horizontal lever that controlled lift and descent and then released the restraining wire. History was about to be made.

The moment was the culmination of years of research into flight that began when Orville and Wilbur's father bought them a windup "helicopter" toy powered by a rubber band. As adults the Wright brothers became flying fanatics, experimenting with the rules of aviation in a home-made wind tunnel and testing out their theories during hundreds of glider flights. The brothers concluded an aircraft would have to be powered by an engine to sustain its lift, and set about building one light enough to sit on a glider fuselage.

On the morning of December 17, 1903, the Flyer rushed along the remote beach at Kitty Hawk and took to the skies. The first sustained powered flight in history was short: the Flyer stayed in the air for 12 seconds and covered a distance of 36m (118ft), but more trials were made that day. During one, Wilbur was able to achieve a successful 59-second flight that covered 259m (850ft). However, the Wright brothers received little recognition for their achievements at the time. Local newspapers reacted with disbelief to their claim, and their secrecy over flying demonstrations led some to label them as "bluffers". Despite building new and better Flyers, it wasn't until 1908 that the Wright brothers' claims achieved legitimacy. Then, thousands flocked to see a series of demonstrations in France that made the brothers world famous overnight. Today, the Wright brothers are remembered as the flight pioneers who developed the first airplane and made it fly.

A Timeline: the Life and Experience of the Wright Brothers

1783 The French Montgolfier brothers carry out the first flight of a hot-air balloon over Paris.

1804 English aviation engineer George Cayley develops a model glider with a fixed main wing.

1853 George Cayley's New Flyer takes his footman across Brompton Dale in the first manned glider flight.

1893 During the first controlled flights in a glider, Otto Lilienthal covers distances of up to 230m (754ft).

1893 The Wright brothers begin to sell and repair bicycles.

1896 The Wright brothers take an active interest in aviation, developing and building gliders in their bicycle workshop.

1900 The Wright brothers begin experimenting with their gliders at Kitty Hawk, North Carolina.

1903 The Wright brothers achieve the first sustained powered flight in history.

1904–1905 The Wright brothers develop a practical airplane near Dayton, Ohio.

1908 The Wright brothers begin to manufacture airplanes.

1909 The Wright brothers demonstrate a two-passenger airplane in Europe and America.

1912 Wilbur Wright dies of typhoid in Dayton, Ohio.

1914–8 Dramatic improvements in aerodynamics – including higher speeds and manoeuvrability – are made to enhance Second World War fighter planes.

1915 Orville Wright sells his interest in the Wright Company.

1919 U.S. Navy aviators make the first airplane crossing of the north Atlantic.

1927 Charles Lindbergh completes the first nonstop solo flight across the Atlantic, traveling 5,796km (3,600 miles) from New York to Paris aboard the *Spirit of St. Louis*.

1933 Boeing introduces the 247, the world's first commercial airplane.

1948 Orville Wright dies and the Wright brothers' 1903 Flyer is enshrined at the Smithsonian Institution.

THE DISCOVERY OF COSMIC RADIO WAVES

1933

"Radio astronomy has, in the last decade, opened a new window on the physical universe. It may also, if we are wise enough to make the effort, cast a brilliant light on the biological universe."

Carl Sagan, 1978.

The first time the dots of light in the night sky resolved into anything else was in 1609, when Galileo built the first telescope capable of revealing the detail of the planets. Galileo had heard of the invention of the telescope in Flanders in 1608 and rushed to make his own, better, model. Instead of 3x magnification, Galileo's telescope had 20x magnification. With it, he could see the surface of the Moon and – more importantly – the rings of Saturn and the moons of Jupiter, and that the planets were physical bodies, perhaps like the Earth. It was the first step towards exploring space.

Large radio telescopes can be single dishes or many dishes and antennae linked together (array telescopes). The Arecibo radio telescope in Puerto Rico has a dish 305m (1,000ft) across. Since its opening in 1963, it has been instrumental in discovering the first evidence of neutron stars, binary pulsars and exoplanets (planets outside our solar system). It is also the base of SETI, the Search for Extra-Terrestrial Intelligence, hunting for evidence of alien intelligence. Array telescopes are used for inferometry, which adds together signals picked up by many antennae, sometimes spread over a large area. They are best for resolving fine detail from bright objects. The Karl G. Jansky Very Large Array in New Mexico has 27 telescopes over a span of 80km (49 miles).

Radio signals from space have numerous sources, including supernovae, pulsars, quasars and galaxy remnants. Monitoring emissions from sources within the solar system enables astonomers to calculate, for example, the temperatures of other planets. Monitoring radio from deep space has led to many discoveries. When Jocelyn Bell discovered a highly regular pulse of radio signals in 1967, she at first suspected that it was a deliberate artificial signal that could be a sign of intelligent life. In fact, it turned out to be the first pulsar – a highly magnetized rotating neutron star.

Both optical and radio telescopes suffer from waves being bent or reflected by the Earth's atmosphere, but telescopes sited on satellites above the atmosphere don't suffer from this problem. The Hubble Space Telescope, a high-resolution optical telescope, was launched in 1990 and has provided thousands of stunning photographs of distant phenomena as well as objects within the solar system. The Russian space-based radio telescope Spektr-R (launched in 2011) is used in conjunction with radio telescopes on Earth using inferometry techniques. Other space-based telescopes operate at the other end of the spectrum, detecting gamma rays or X-rays.

Visible light forms only a tiny portion of the electromagnetic spectrum. As we see light beamed through space every day, it is hardly surprising that other types of electromagnetic radiation also reach us, though it was not thought possible at first.

In 1931, Karl Jansky was investigating interference on long-distance voice transmissions for Bell Telephone Laboratories when he found a persistent hiss that was most pronounced at about the same time each day. He ruled out thunderstorms and even the sun, as he found that the repeat cycle was 23 hours and 56 minutes – the same as Earth's rotation relative to the stars. Recognizing that the signal came from space, he consulted star maps and identified the source as somewhere near the centre of the galaxy. He announced his astonishing discovery in 1933, but Bell refused his request for funding to build a radio telescope.

Four years later in September 1937, Illinois-born Grote Reber built the first radio telescope in his back garden. It was made up of a parabolic sheet-metal mirror 9m (30ft) in diameter, focusing to a radio receiver 8m (26ft) above the mirror. The telescope was mounted on a tilting stand that allowed it to be pointed in different directions, although not actually turned. It took him three attempts, but eventually Reber managed to construct a telescope that could detect signals from outer space.

Ever since then, radio telescopes have profoundly changed what we know about the universe. They focus incoming electromagnetic radiation on an antenna, then convert the signal to a tiny electric current, which is recorded. The strength and frequency of the signal are measured. If or when we discover life elsewhere in the universe, it will be a radio telescope that finds the signal.

———◦◦✕◦◦———

A Timeline: the Before, During and After of the First Radio

1608 The first optical telescopes (those that work with light) are made in the Netherlands.

1609 Galileo uses a telescope to see details of the moon and planets for the first time.

1896 Johannes Wilsing and Julius Scheiner attempt to pick up radio emissions from the Sun, but fail.

1902 Physicists conclude that radio waves from space would bounce back off the Earth's atmosphere and be undetectable.

1932 Karl Jansky realizes that radio interference on voice signals is coming from distant space.

1937 Grote Reber builds a 9m (30ft) parabolic dish radio telescope in his back garden.

1963 Quasars are discovered by Maarten Schmidt.

1963 The Arecibo observatory opens in Puerto Rico.

1964 Arno Penzias and Robert Wilson discover cosmic microwave background radiation.

1967 Jocelyn Bell discovers the first pulsar from its extremely regular pulses every 1.33 seconds.

1990 The Hubble Space Telescope is launched into orbit around the Earth.

2011 The Russian satellite radio telescope Spektr-R is launched.

2015 Breakthrough Listen is launched, a massive international project to look for radio signals that indicate life elsewhere in the universe. It targets the nearest million stars, the nearest hundred galaxies, and the core of the Milky Way.

JOHN LOGIE BAIRD SHOWS TV TO THE WORLD

1926

"The image of the dummy's head formed itself on the screen
with what appeared to be almost unbelievable clarity...
I ran down the little flight of stairs to Mr Cross's office and
seized by the arm his office boy William Taynton, hauled him
upstairs and put him in front of the transmitter."

John Logie Baird describes the moment he first successfully
transmitted moving images.

In 1923, the engineer and inventor John Logie Baird built the world's first-ever television set from a hatbox, a pair of scissors, a tea chest, some bicycle lights and the motor from an electric fan in his workshop. He used his TV set to transmit moving silhouette images, but burned his hand badly when his equipment gave him a 1,000-volt electric shock. Baird was subsequently invited to vacate his Hastings workshop following the incident and relocated to a new laboratory in Soho, London, where he continued his work.

From his Soho laboratory, Baird successfully transmitted moving images: first of a ventriloquist dummy and then a 20-year-old office worker called William Edward Taynton. Excited by the breakthrough, Baird visited the offices of the *Daily Express* newspaper to publicize his new invention. In response, the disbelieving news editor of the paper ordered a reporter to escort Baird from the building, saying, "For God's sake, go down to reception and get rid of a lunatic who's down there. He says he's got a machine for seeing by wireless! Watch him – he may have a razor on him."

In 1928, John Logie Baird founded the Baird Television Development Company Ltd, which wowed people in Britain and the United States by making the first transatlantic television transmission from London to New York. Baird then made the first-ever television program for the BBC. Next, Baird devised a way of capturing live events, and televised the Epsom Derby in 1931. He later constructed a theatre-projection system to televise a boxing match on a giant 4.6-by-3.7m (15-by-12ft) screen.

In 1929, the BBC used Baird's television system to broadcast its programs, but from 1936 began alternating between Baird's transmission system and Marconi–EMI's system. The BBC then decided to test both systems alongside each other in a six-month trial. But disaster struck in 1937, when much of Baird's equipment was destroyed in a fire at his London laboratory. The BBC then decided that the Baird system was inadequate because of the lack of mobility posed by its large cameras, hoses, developing tanks and cables. Baird's television systems were then replaced by the electronic television system developed by Marconi–EMI. As the BBC began a regular TV service, the television age began – but it would take place without Baird.

❧

On January 26, 1926, members of the Royal Commission and the press were invited to an upper-floor laboratory in Soho, London. According to an attending *Times* reporter, the men had been invited for a "demonstration of apparatus invented by Mr J.L. Baird, who claims to have solved the problem of television." Scottish inventor John Logie Baird called his apparatus the "televisor", and its invention would launch a revolution in communication and entertainment that is today used by billions of people worldwide.

Baird's televisor used mechanical rotating disks to scan images into electronic signals and transmit them to a screen. To demonstrate this process to the Royal Commission, Baird filmed himself playing with two ventriloquist dummy heads that he then produced on a screen in front of his audience. Baird had based his televisor on the work of scientist Paul Nipkow, who created an earlier television system using rotating disks but had failed to create a discernible image on screen. By improving on Nipkow's design, Baird was able to stun the world by successfully transmitting moving pictures through the phone line from London to Glasgow in 1927. In 1928, Baird transmitted the first TV pictures from Britain to America via undersea cables, and later that year produced the first color images, which included strawberries and a man in a red-and-white scarf. But Baird was not the only inventor working on televisions. In 1936, the BBC (British Broadcasting Corporation) began its first television service and tested Baird's system alongside an electronic design created by Marconi Electric and Musical Industries (EMI).

In the end, the Marconi–EMI system was found to be more efficient and won out over Baird's televisor. Despite the setback, Baird continued to work on his television inventions and reportedly developed an early 3D television before his death in 1946.

———◦◦◇◦◦———

A Timeline: the Life, Experience and Influence of the John Logie Baird

1873 Willoughby Smith discovers selenium, which was used to transform pictures into electrical signals.

1880 Alexander Graham Bell and Thomas Edison invent the Photophone, a device they hope will transfer pictures as well as sound.

1884 German inventor Paul Nipkow patents the Nipkow Disk, a spinning disk that uses a pattern of holes to scan an image.

1897 K.F. Braun invents the cathode-ray tube, which is later used in all modern televisions.

1922 Vladimir Kosmich Zworykin patents his iconoscope television transmission tube.

1925 American inventor Charles Jenkins publicly demonstrates the transmission of moving silhouette images.

1928 Television is introduced in the United States.

1928 American W2XB becomes the first television station in the world.

1928 The first commercial television set, "The Daven", is sold for $75.

1929 The German Post Office asks John Logie Baird to develop an experimental television service.

1930 Charles Jenkins broadcasts the first-ever TV commercial.

1936 The BBC introduces the world's first television service, which broadcasts three hours of programming a day.

1944 John Logie Baird gives the world's first demonstration of an electronic color television display.

1944 The world's first 625-line television is designed in the Soviet Union.

1946 John Logie Baird dies.

1948 The number of television sets in American homes reaches one million.

1950 Color TV is released to the public.

1960 Seventy-five percent of British homes have a television set.

TURING: TOWARDS THINKING MACHINES

1936

"Turing's paper...contains, in essence, the invention of the modern computer and some of the programming techniques that accompanied it."

Marvin Minsky, 1967.

In 1936, Alan Turing described an "a-machine" (or "automatic machine"), a hypothetical machine that acts as a blueprint for any computer. It would read data from a paper tape and manipulate it following a set of instructions (a program). Turing proposed that given enough memory and time, any computational task could be carried out – it just had to be expressed as rules (algorithms). The combination of memory, program, processing, input and output has come to define all subsequent computers. He also proposed that a powerful enough a-machine (now called a "universal Turing machine") would be able to emulate any other computer as it just needs to follow instructions to behave in the same way. This was revolutionary at a time when machines were designed to tackle a single task.

Turing's challenge for computer intelligence has become known as the "Turing Test". It requires a human interrogator to question, by text, two other "subjects", one a human and the other a computer. The computer passes the test if the interrogator cannot identify the computer 70 percent of the time after a five-minute "conversation".

An early natural-language program, ELIZA, written by Joseph Weizenbaum in 1966, examined patterns in speech to respond to human remarks with apparently apt questions. One version successfully imitated a therapist, responding to remarks as "My mother hates me" with, "Who else in your family hates you?" A number of people were fooled, believing ELIZA showed genuine intelligence.

The field of artificial intelligence (AI) was first defined by John McCarthy in 1955. One problem that besets research and development in AI is that there is no agreed definition of intelligence of any type. Theories of human and animal intelligence prioritize different aspects. Which definition of intelligence is to be emulated? Further, there is no single approach to developing machine intelligence, with some researchers wishing to emulate human intelligence and working from neurology and psychology, while others look for completely novel ways of constructing intelligence. As they point out, we don't model planes on the way birds fly, so why should we try to copy the working of the human brain to produce intelligence?

Games were one early approach to intelligence, and even Turing had played around writing a computer program to play chess (though only on paper). Now, the most sophisticated chess programs can beat any human – that barrier was broken in 1997, when IBM's Deep Blue defeated the reigning world chess-champion, Gary Kasparov. But Deep Blue is more an "expert system" than genuinely intelligent. Expert systems search and collate a massive dataset, try out many solutions very rapidly, and some "learn" from past mistakes, but they can't go beyond their initial programming and knowledge base.

Alan Turing (1912–54) is in many senses the father of modern computing. He proposed a theoretical model for a programmable computer in 1936, which has since come to be seen as the foundation of subsequent actual computers. Now called the "Turing machine", his idea described a machine capable of performing any calculations by following a series of logical instructions.

During the Second World War, Turing worked at Bletchley Park, the codebreaking centre in England. He was instrumental in developing technology to crack the coding of a German encryption machine known as Enigma. The de-encryption machine, the "bombe", is credited with shortening the war by up to four years. After the war, Turing worked at the National Physical Laboratory, where he designed ACE, one of the first stored-program digital computers. In 1948, he moved to Manchester University, where pioneering work in computing was being carried out.

There, in 1950, he published a groundbreaking paper, "Computing Machinery and Intelligence", in which he suggested the highly provocative idea that a computer could be designed that could learn and then think independently. He formulated a test for such a computer, which a computer could pass if it were able to fool a human interrogator into believing it was human.

This test, known as the "Turing Test", has been explored extensively since 1950 and is still a subject of popular debate today.

A Timeline: the Life, Experience and Influence of Alan Turing

1770 Wolfgang von Kempelen introduces his chess-playing automaton, the Mechanical Turk – but it is a hoax, with a human chess player hidden inside.

1912 Alan Turing is born in London.

1936 Turing suggests his theoretical model for an a-machine (automatic machine) and for a universal Turing machine.

1943 Colossus, the first electric, digital, programmable computer, is demonstrated at Bletchley Park; it is used to crack the German Lorenz cipher and is kept secret.

1950 Alan Turing publishes "Computing Machinery and Intelligence".

1951 Dietrich Prinz develops the first computer chess program, though it can only solve short chess problems rather than play a whole game.

1954 Turing takes a lethal dose of cyanide after prosecution and punishment for homosexual acts.

1955 John McCarthy coins the term "artificial intelligence" to denote "the science and engineering of making intelligent machines".

1958 The chess program NSS defeats a novice human chess player, the first time a computer outwits a human being.

1966 Joseph Weizenbaum creates ELIZA, the first natural-language processing program that can hold a type of conversation with humans.

1974 The existence of Colossus is finally revealed, 30 years later.

1997 Chess grand master Garry Kasparov is beaten by an IBM computer playing chess.

2011 Apple introduces Siri, the "intelligent personal assistant", as part of iOS 5. on iPhones.

ALTAIR 8800: THE DAWN OF PERSONAL COMPUTING

1975

"There is no reason for any individual
to have a computer in his home."

Ken Olson, founder of Digital Equipment Corporation, 1977.

The idea that a machine could take over some of our mental work is old. Blaise Pascal built the "Pascaline" mechanical calculator in 1642, prompted by Pascal helping his father with burdensome calculations as a supervisor of taxes. In 1801, the jacquard loom stored complex weaving patterns on punched cards – the first use of "programming", though the machine was entirely mechanical. Around 20 years later, Charles Babbage put calculating and program together, at least in theory. He designed two machines in the 1820s that followed programmed instructions, written for Babbage by Ava Lovelace, but did not have the funds to build them.

The claim to being the first programmable computer actually built is hotly contested. Konrad Zuse built the Z1 in 1936–8, though it and its construction plans were destroyed in the Second World War by Allied air raids on Berlin in 1943. It was a partially programmable calculator. The war also saw the development of Colossus at Bletchley Park in England, built to crack German secret codes in 1943. The work was top secret, and the machines and plans for them were destroyed after the war. With everyone who worked on it sworn to secrecy for decades, Colossus was generally overshadowed by the later American military computer, ENIAC, built in 1946.

The kit computers such as the Altair 8800 appealed to enthusiasts, but as soon as manufacturers began to produce ready-built computers with a keyboard and monitor, that would do useful things, personal computers took off in the mainstream. Initially, there was no conformity – one computer was not compatible with another, and they all used different operating systems and required different programs. By the end of the 1980s, though, this had resolved into the dominance of the IBM-PC and Apple, with other manufacturers largely switching to PC-compatible products in order to survive.

The next big change was the development of the graphical user interface (GUI), the familiar desktop with windows, icons and documents, navigated using a mouse and menus. The original concept was designed at Xerox Park, as an experimental idea for use on large computers, but was soon copied (Xerox claimed stolen) by Apple. The Apple Lisa, released in 1983, was the first computer to use a GUI. The interface was used for other Apple computers, and emulated in the form of Windows for PC-compatible computers in 1985. The new interface made computers easier to use – no one needed to remember strings of apparently meaningless commands – and their appeal rapidly widened to even the least technically sophisticated of home users.

Personal computers, and their progeny in the form of smartphones, tablets and other "devices", are a feature of everyday life. Yet it is little more than 40 years since the very first personal computer hit the shops. Or, actually, the mail-order listings in hobby magazines. It could be bought pre-assembled, or as a build-it-yourself kit. Once it was built, the owner had to program it. And reprogram it every time it was turned on, as it didn't have any means of storing programs or data. Nor did it have an easy way of entering or examining them, as there was no keyboard, screen or mouse.

The first personal computer was the Altair 8800, launched in 1975. It was programmed by flicking switches and showed its results by flashing lights. It could be built in any box the enthusiast had handy. Despite these limitations, it was hugely popular. Ed Roberts, who designed and made the Altair kits, expected to sell only a few hundred but in fact sold several thousand in the first month after it was featured in the January issue of Popular Electronics. The first programming language for the Altair was Altair BASIC – the first product of the new company Micro-Soft (it had a hyphen in those days). Both the idea of a personal computer, and Microsoft, took off.

It was not a smooth ride from the Altair to the present, though. Initially, a host of small computer companies set up business, many starting in garages in California, as Apple did. Each of these came up with its own architecture for hardware and software and the result was myriad incompatible systems. The move towards conformity began only when IBM introduced its own personal computer in 1981. Over the coming years, other systems were slowly squeezed out of the market, leaving only Apple with its own proprietary system and the industry-standard IBM-PC running MS DOS. Although MS DOS came to be used on a large number of PC-clones, Apple kept the rights to its operating system for its own computers – a distinction it still maintains.

A Timeline: the Before, During and After of the First Personal Computer

1642 Blaise Pascal invents the Pascaline, a mechanical calculator.

1801 The jacquard loom is the first machine to be controlled by punched cards with coded instructions.

1820s Charles Babbage designs but does not build his Difference Engine and Analytical Engine, two mechanical programmable computers.

1936–8 Konrad Zuse builds an electro-mechanical programmable computer, the Z1.

1943 Colossus, built secretly at Bletchley Park in England, is the first programmable electronic computer.

1948 "Baby", the first stored-program computer, is built in Manchester, England.

1951 Maurice Wilkes develops "microprogramming" to control different aspects of the computer itself, effectively separating the operating system from other programs.

1975 The Altair 8800 goes on sale, the first-ever personal computer.

1975 Micro-Soft (later Microsoft) is founded by Bill Gates to produce BASIC for the Altair 8800.

1976 Steve Jobs, Steve Wozniak and Robert Wayne found Apple to sell the Apple I computer kit.

1980–1 Microsoft produce MS-DOS for the forthcoming IBM PC.

1981 IBM PC is launched, with the cheapest model selling for $1,565 with no disk drives.

1983 The graphical user interface makes its first appearance on the Apple Lisa.

1990 The launch of the World Wide Web.

THE WORLD WIDE WEB

1991

"A 'web' of notes with links between them is far more useful than a fixed hierarchical system."

Tim Berners-Lee, in his proposal for the World Wide Web.

The World Wide Web is built on the internet, which grew from ARPANET. ARPANET was first proposed in 1967, and developed by the Advanced Research Projects Agency (ARPA) from U.S. defense funding. In October 1969, ARPANET began by linking two computers in California – one at UCLA and the other at SRI – allowing researchers to share information long distance. It used a packet-switching protocol, which means that instead of a dedicated connection (like a phone line), communications are chopped into chunks, or packets, that are sent over shared connections and put back together at their destination. ARPANET soon expanded its reach, with other universities and research facilities linking in to the network. In 1973, the first computers outside the U.S.A. linked to ARPANET, beginning with computers in Norway and then England.

ARPANET was not the only network. More networks grew up, both in the U.S. and elsewhere. In 1981, access to ARPANET was expanded and the following year the TCP/IP protocol provided a standardized method for computers to communicate. The concept of a worldwide network of computers all communicating with each other became fully realizable. Other networks linked to ARPANET, and in 1983 the internet was born, with ARPANET now just a part of it. The emergence of commercial internet providers during the 1990s made it fully available to commercial enterprises and even individuals.

The start of the next phase of the web has begun, the "Internet of Things". More and more devices are connected to the internet, but so far most of these have had human users behind them. The Internet of Things involves objects that have direct access to and interaction with the internet on their own, through automation rather than a personal choice to connect. The first internet "thing" was a modified Coca Cola dispenser that, in 1982, could upload its inventory and show whether newly loaded drinks were cold. Wireless connections and miniaturization have made it possible for more things to be internet-connected. Predictions suggest that 20–50 billion "things" will be connected by 2020.

The web was slow to take off with the public until the web browser Mosaic (1993) and early search engines made it easy to find and view web pages. Use of the web then grew steadily over the course of the 1990s. In 1994, there were 2,738 websites and around 45 million internet users; in 2000, there were over 17 million websites and over 400 million internet users. As the web grew, its focus began to change. In the early years of the 21st century, "Web 2.0" began to emerge. This is a more dynamic interactive form of the web, in which ordinary users contribute content on social networking and file-sharing sites, and through blogs and wikis.

It's difficult to imagine life without the World Wide Web now, yet it's been with us for less that 30 years, and in its early years it was used by relatively few people. The web was developed at CERN, the European Organization for Nuclear Research, in Switzerland, by Tim Berners-Lee. Frustrated at the difficulty of sharing documents with colleagues working in the same area, he proposed a system for computers to share text and photographs with links between them, so that people could easily follow cross-references. He wasn't given permission to develop it as a CERN project, but pursued it on his own.

The early web was used first within CERN, and then with other research establishments and universities. Information kept on one computer used hypertext links to call up information kept on another computer, the two being linked by the internet. The first web page went live in 1991; it had links to the other 25 pages on the web. There are now more than five billion web pages.

Initially, the web was used only at academic and other research institutions. It became more widely accessible as better web browsers and search engines were developed. The first web browser to catch the public imagination was Mosaic, launched in 1993. It was the first browser to display text and pictures on the same page, rather then having all images open in a separate window. It was compatible with PCs, which by 1993 dominated home and business markets. That year also saw the first precursor of a search engine, called W3Catalog. It was not a real search engine, but a catalogue of the websites available. One of the first search engines that "crawled" the web, building a database of content that could be properly searched, was WebCrawler, released in 1994. Search engines quickly proliferated. With a way of displaying text and images together, and a way to search for content, the web's popularity began its meteoric rise.

—◇◇◇◇◇—

A Timeline: the Life, Experience and Influence of the World Wide Web

1945 Vannevar Bush publishes his ideas for a machine that presents information in a linked form, and predicts an "information explosion" later in the century.

1963 ASCII code is developed as a way of representing text that all computers can interpret.

1969 ARPANET links two computers in the U.S.A.

1971 Ray Tomlinson sends the first email.

1973 Norway and England gain links to ARPANET, the first outside the U.S. to connect to it.

1973 FTP is implemented, allowing file transfer over the network.

1974 The term "internet" is first used.

1978 Ward Christensen develops CBBS, a bulletin-board system to share news online.

1980 The Usenet news-sharing system is set up, presenting news and comments in threads.

1982 A modified Coca-Cola dispenser becomes the first item to upload information about itself.

1983 TCP/IP becomes the new protocol for traffic, and ARPANET becomes only part of the network, now the internet.

1989 Tim Berners-Lee proposes developing a web of information.

1990 ARPANET is officially decommissioned.

1991 The first web page is launched.

1993 The first popular web browser, Mosaic, is developed.

1994 The first search engine, WebCrawler, is developed, which could search the text of all web pages.

1999 Wireless, mobile email arrives with the BlackBerry.

2004 The term "Web 2.0" is coined to describe the new face of the web that lets users upload resources and contribute to online activity.

MEDICINE

The Identification of Blood Groups

Development of Antibiotics

First Successful Organ Transplant

The Vaccine that Saved a Nation's Children (Polio)

IVF: the First Test-tube Baby

THE IDENTIFICATION OF BLOOD GROUPS

1901

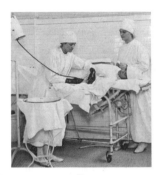

"The reactions follow a pattern, which is valid for the blood of all humans...Basically, in fact, there are four different types of human blood, the so-called blood groups."

Karl Landsteiner, in a lecture accepting his Nobel Prize in 1930
(translated by Pauline M.H. Mazumdar).

The earliest attempts at blood transfusions moved blood between animals, and then between humans and animals. An infusion of animal blood can cause a fatal allergic reaction, but when only small amounts of blood were used this did not always happen. Dr Jean-Baptiste Denys successfully transfused sheep blood into two patients who survived, but two later patients, one transfused with blood from a calf, died. Attempts at transfusion stopped for around 150 years. Interest in it grew again in the early 19th century, with some successful human-to-human transfusions. It was risky, though, as it frequently led to problems.

Why should transfusions sometimes go well and sometimes be disastrous? This puzzled medical researchers until Karl Landsteiner's ground-breaking discoveries. If a person is given incompatible blood, their body's immune system attacks the new blood cells, which first form clumps and then disintegrate. The blood groups Landsteiner identified were A, which has A-antigens inside red blood cells and B-antibodies in the plasma; B, which has B-antigens in the cells and A-antibodies in the plasma; and C (now called O), which has no antigens in the cells and both types of antibodies in the plasma. AB, discovered later, has both types of antigens in the red blood cells and no antibodies. Antibodies are in the blood plasma (the liquid that carries the blood cells), which is no longer used in transfusions.

Blood grouping has more uses than transfusion. In 1910–1, Ludwik Hirszfeld and Emil von Dungern discovered that ABO blood group is an inherited characteristic, and in 1924 Felix Bernstein demonstrated the slightly complex pattern of inheritance. This made it possible to use blood grouping to help establish – or disprove – paternity. On a larger scale, studying the blood groups of entire populations can give an indication of migration patterns in the past. This was discovered near the end of the First World War, when Hanna and Ludwig Hirszfeld found a sharp drop in A-type blood at the German border with Poland.

Understanding blood groups enabled blood transfusions and made possible more complicated surgery. The first human-to-human transfusion was in 1906, and involved having the donor alongside the recipient. Transfusions of blood that had already been taken from the donor began in 1914 – just in time for the First World War, but blood could not be preserved long enough for transfusions to be widespread. By the end of the war, soldiers in some armies wore tags that gave their blood group, speeding up the process of finding compatible blood, if injured. Blood could be kept for a short time using sodium citrate to prevent clotting. From 1930, the red blood cells were removed from the plasma and could be kept for longer.

Surgery beyond simple amputations was made possible in the 19th century through the development of anaesthetics and antiseptics, but blood loss could still cause death. Early attempts to give blood transfusions usually failed. Karl Landsteiner found out why, making blood transfusions reliable and saving millions of lives over the last century.

Landsteiner investigated the effect of mixing animal and human blood, and often blood from two different human subjects. He found that it frequently led to the red blood cells clumping, then sometimes breaking apart, releasing haemoglobin into the blood. This is dangerous, and can be fatal. It did not always happen, though: sometimes he could mix blood from different people without the cells clumping.

Blood comprises red blood cells, white blood cells and plasma – a pale yellow fluid. Through his experiments, Landsteiner found in 1901 that it was something in the plasma that caused problems with the blood cells. If he mixed red blood cells with incompatible blood plasma, the clumping (agglutination) occurred. He worked out that blood falls into different groups, some of which are compatible and some not. He divided blood into groups A, B and C (now known as O). He discovered that blood of the same group does not cause problems, and group O (or C) can accept groups A and B – but A and B cannot accept O. Alfred von Decastello and Adriano Sturli discovered the fourth type, AB, in 1902. People with AB-group blood can accept any type of blood, but AB blood can only be given to AB patients.

The first successful blood transfusion followed in 1906, carried out by George Washington Crile in Cleveland, USA, using matched blood groups. Other distinctions between blood types have been found since Landsteiner's basic groups. More than 30 systems of blood grouping are now known.

———∞◇∞———

A Timeline: the Before, During and After of the Identification of Blood Groups

1665 Richard Lower demonstrates blood transfusion between two living dogs to the Royal Society in London. Both survive.

1667 Jean-Baptiste Denys successfully transfuses blood from a sheep to a 15-year-old boy.

1668 The Royal Society in Britain, and the French government, ban further experiments with blood transfusion.

1670 The Vatican condemns blood transfusion.

1818 Dr James Blundell carries out the first successful human-to-human blood transfusion to treat bleeding after childbirth.

1840 Samuel Armstrong Lane, helped by Blundell, carries out the first whole transfusion to treat hemophilia.

1875 Leonard Landois reported that mixing blood from other animals with human blood caused blood cells to clump together and sometimes break up.

1901 Karl Landsteiner discovers that blood falls into different groups that are partially incompatible; he names these A, B and O.

1902 Alfred von Decastello and Adriano Sturli define an additional blood group, AB.

1902 Lansdsteiner and Max Richter explain how blood groups can be used in forensics, identifying the group of even dried blood found at a crime scene.

1906 George Washington Crile oversees the first surgery involving direct blood transfusion (i.e. with the donor present and connected to the recipient).

1910–11 Ludwik Hirszfeld and Emil von Dungern show that blood groups are inherited.

1914 Belgian doctor Albert Hustin performs a non-direct transfusion using diluted blood.

1917 The first blood banks are set up in preparation for the Battle of Ypres in the First World War.

1921 The first blood-donation service is started by Percy Oliver, secretary of the British Red Cross.

1930 In the U.S.S.R., Vladimir Shamov and Sergei Yudin pioneer the use of blood from recently dead corpses.

1939 It is discovered that matched blood groups can still cause clotting.

1940 Landsteiner and Alexander Wiener identify the Rhesus factor in blood groups.

DEVELOPMENT OF ANTIBIOTICS

1928

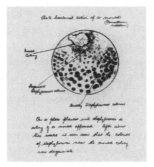

"I have been trying to point out that in our lives chance may have an astonishing influence and, if I may offer advice to the young laboratory worker, it would be this – never neglect an extraordinary appearance or happening."

Sir Alexander Fleming, on his accidental discovery.

Before the development of antibiotics, even seemingly minor injuries and infections could prove serious or even fatal. If the body's immune system was not sufficiently robust to defeat invading bacteria, the outlook was grim. From the earliest times, people had used honey and oil on wounds – excluding air prevented infection by aerobic bacteria (those that need oxygen). Packing wounds with moss, initially probably intended as a dressing, also sometimes prevented infection, as the moss contained chemicals with antibiotic properties – but no one knew they were there, so it was rather hit and miss. The search for antibiotics began in earnest once the development of anaesthetics extended the potential of surgery. Once the pain was removed, infection was the largest barrier.

The German chemist Gerhard Domagk had been experimenting with the dye prontosil rubrum when, in 1935, his six-year-old daughter pricked her finger on a knitting needle and developed a serious infection. The recommended treatment was amputation of the arm to try to prevent her death. Domagk knew that prontosil had antibiotic effects in mice, but it had never been tried with humans before. Desperate, he treated his daughter with it and she recovered. Prontosil and other sulfa drugs became immensely popular and saved many lives during the Second World War, but their frequent side effects meant that they were quickly replaced by later antibiotics.

Although Domagk's daughter suffered her infection after Fleming's discovery of penicillin, it had not yet been developed into a medicine. That was achieved by Howard Florcy and Ernst Chain in 1945. They, too, found that it was impossible to produce penicillin in large enough quantities from *Penicillium notatum*. They had succeeded in 1940 in delaying the death of their first patient, but then ran out of penicillin and he died anyway. After a worldwide search for a better mould for extracting penicillin, they finally found a source that yielded a thousand times that of Fleming's mould. Production started in vast towers in the U.S., as English factories had been commandeered for the war effort. By 1945, 650 billion units were being produced each month.

Bacteria adapt and evolve quickly, and it was not long before many bacteria developed resistance to penicillin: the wonder-drug no longer worked as well as it once had. The barrier to making variants of penicillin was understanding the structure of the molecule involved. The new technique of X-ray crystallography offered a chance. The complex task of breaking down the molecule, building an image of its components using X-ray crystallography, and then piecing them back together was finally accomplished by Dorothy Hodgkin in 1945. Armed with the knowledge of penicillin's molecular structure, chemists were able to manufacture effective artificial forms of penicillin and make new antibiotics.

Antibiotics are one of the most important developments of the 20th century. They have saved millions of lives and yet their discovery was accidental.

The first modern antibiotic to be discovered and produced in large quantities was penicillin. The story of its accidental discovery by Alexander Fleming is well known. In 1928, Fleming took a holiday from work in his laboratory, piling up used petri dishes before he went, but not cleaning them out (he was notoriously untidy). His poor housekeeping was serendipitous. When he returned a couple of weeks later, his discarded dishes were still there. But there were clear spaces where the colony of the *Staphylococcus* bacteria he was growing had died. Investigation revealed that a mould had grown on the plates – *Penicillium notatum* – and this had killed the bacteria. Fleming found that the mould would kill a number of bacteria, including those causing diphtheria, scarlet fever, pneumonia and meningitis. He couldn't produce penicillin in large enough quantities to use as medicine, and he believed that its action was so slow that it would not remain in the body long enough to have an effect.

Ernst Chain and Howard Florey took up where Fleming had left off in 1938. They made a medicine from penicillin which they first tried in 1940 on a patient who had developed an infection after being injured gardening and was close to death. He began to improve, but after five days the supply of penicillin ran out and he died.

In 1941, Chain and Florey were working in the U.S.A when a laboratory assistant bought a melon infested with *Penicillium chrysogeum*. It turned out to produce 200 times as much penicillin as *Penicillium notatum*. After processing, it became the source of large enough supplies of penicillin to save many Allied lives in the Second World War.

———◦◦◦◦◦◦———

A Timeline: the Before, During and After of the Development of Antibiotics

1896 Ernest Duchesne discovers penicillin while a final-year student at the Pasteur Institute in Paris, but it goes unnoticed.

1860–4 Louis Pasteur demonstrates that bacteria can cause disease – the first formal evidence of germ theory.

1909 Paul Ehrlich and Sahachiro Hata develop Salvarsan to treat syphilis. It is the first treatment targeted at a specific organism, calculated to affect it using detailed scientific knowledge – a "magic bullet" for a specific condition.

1915 Frederick Twort discovers phages – viruses that attack bacteria.

1923 The Eliava Institute is founded in Georgia, U.S.S.R., to study the use of phages as a means of controlling bacterial disease.

1928 Alexander Fleming accidentally discovers the antibacterial effect of the mould *Penicillium notatum* on *Staphylococcus aureus*.

1935 Gerhard Domagk uses the dye prontosil rubrum on his desperately ill young daughter, saving her life. This was the first sulfa drug.

1937 Around 100 people are poisoned by contaminated sulfa drugs, prompting the introduction of testing and quality control for medicines.

1941 Howard Florey and Ernst Chain complete the first human trials of penicillin.

1943 Albert Schatz discovers the antibiotic streptomycin; it is soon in production being used to treat tuberculosis.

1945 Dorothy Hodgkin uncovers the molecular structure of penicillin, using X-ray diffraction.

1961 The first reported appearance of MRSA (methicillin-resistant *Staphylococcus aureus*).

1986 The first monoclonal antibody is produced. Monoclonal antibodies target a single, specific disease.

1990 Antibiotic-resistant disease is expected to contribute to ten million deaths a year – more than cancer.

FIRST SUCCESSFUL ORGAN TRANSPLANT

1954

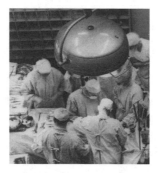

"It is infinitely better to transplant a heart than to bury it to be devoured by worms."

Christiaan Barnard, the first surgeon
to perform a heart transplant.

There are a few, probably apocryphal, accounts of early transplants, but the first that is likely to be true… is a bone transplant from a dog to patch the injured skull of a Russian soldier in 1668. Assuming the bone was thoroughly cleaned of all dog tissue, this would be no less likely to succeed than patching the skull with metal. Skin grafts using the recipient's own skin have been used since the ninth century in India to rebuild noses and treat burns and wounds. This ran into no problems of rejection since the skin (still attached by a flap to its former mooring place) was the patient's own. The first attempts at organ transplant were less successful…

In 1909, a French surgeon tried to save a child with kidney failure by inserting slices of rabbit kidney, but the child died after a few days. Similar attempts with kidneys from other animals were equally unsuccessful. During this period, though, Alexis Carrell was pioneering techniques in suturing at a sufficiently small scale to connect blood vessels and nerves, which would be essential in later transplants. Karl Landsteiner's discovery of blood groups removed another hurdle, and the development of antibiotics offered protection against post-operative infection. But attempts at organ transplant continued to fail until the experience of Ronald and Richard Herrick highlighted the role of the immune system in rejection.

The Herrick kidney transplant was the first success, but the first heart transplant is the most famous transplant story of the 20th century. In 1967, South African surgeon Christiaan Barnard transplanted the heart of Denise Darvall, who had died in an accident, into 54-year-old Louis Washkansky. It worked. Unfortunately, after just 18 days, Washkansky died of pneumonia that his suppressed immune system could not combat successfully. The heart had continued to function, though: the problem to sort out was to do with the anti-rejection medication. Once cyclosporine became available in the 1980s, more and more successful transplants of different and multiple organs followed.

The limiting factor for transplants became the supply of organs. In 2008, doctors tried to combine the two fields of organ transplant and regenerative medicine, in the world's first transplant of a regenerated airway. The scaffold for the airway came from a donor, but bone marrow cells from the patient were used to seed the scaffold. This meant that the tissue grown on the scaffold was the patient's own and so anti-rejection drugs were not needed. This was the first organ transplant that did not need anti-rejection drugs and was also not between identical twins. The same technique, but using a synthetic scaffold, was successful in 2011. No anti-rejection drugs are needed with a synthetic scaffold and there is no need to wait for a donor.

For organ transplants to work, we now know, the recipient's body must be receptive to the donated organ. This knowledge comes from the first successful kidney transplant, carried out in 1954. Ronald Herrick donated a kidney to his brother Richard. The secret to the success was in their genetic makeup: Ronald and Richard were identical twins, so Richard's immune system accepted Ronald's kidney rather than rejecting it. Identical twins share the same DNA, so to the immune system, Richard's and Ronald's kidneys were indistinguishable. Richard lived a further eight years after the operation.

Prior to the Herricks' experience, the French surgeon Jean Hamburger carried out a transplant in 1952, using a kidney from the patient's mother. The organ was rejected after three weeks, the recipient's body treating it as foreign matter and setting out to destroy it. After the success of the Herrick transplant, scientists turned to finding a method of calming the immune system. The result was anti-rejection drugs, the most successful of which, cyclosporine, was developed in 1972. The difficulty with anti-rejection drugs, though, is that because they suppress the immune system, the patient is put in danger of contracting other diseases and being unable to fight them off. Transplant patients must take anti-rejection drugs for the rest of their lives. However, in spite of the considerable and ongoing difficulties, there is no doubt that organ transplants have provided hope to millions who would otherwise have been resigned to death.

———◦∞◊∞◦———

A Timeline: the Before, During and After of the First Organ Transplant

1668 A collection of case histories compiled by Dutch physician Job van Meekeren claims that a Russian surgeon has managed the first dog to human skin graft.

1881 A skin graft from a dead body helps heal a man burned by leaning against a metal door as it was struck by lightning.

1901 Karl Landsteiner identifies different blood groups.

1905 Dr Eduard Zirm performs a successful cornea transplant, restoring the sight of a farm laborer blinded in an accident.

1908 Alexis Carrell perfects the fine stitching needed for joining blood vessels in transplant surgery.

1936 Yuri Voronoy in the U.S.S.R. performs a human-to-human kidney transplant, but the recipient dies after two days.

1940s Zoologist Peter Medawar experiments with skin grafts with animals and discovers that an immune response leads to rejection.

1954 The first successful kidney transplant takes place.

1962 The first kidney transplant from a dead donor takes place.

1963 The first successful lung transplant takes place.

1967 Christiaan Barnard carries out the first heart transplant.

1972 The anti-rejection drug cyclosporine is developed; it is first used in 1980.

1981 The first successful heart-lung transplant takes place.

1984 The heart of a young baboon is successfully transplanted into "Baby Fae", but she dies of liver failure 20 days later.

2005 The first face transplant is given to Isabelle Dinoire, whose face had been badly mauled by a dog.

2008 The first transplanted airway using tissue grown from the recipient's own stem cells is performed.

THE VACCINE THAT SAVED A NATION'S CHILDREN (POLIO)

1955

"I have studied the effects of our new lots of polio
vaccine…and…shall give it to my wife and two children
as well as to our neighbors and their children."

Albert Sabin, 1957.

Louis Pasteur developed a vaccine for chicken cholera in 1879 and
for the rabies virus in 1885, successfully treating a young boy after
he had been bitten by a rabid dog. The principle of making vaccines
has remained the same since his time: to isolate the pathogen
and then make a form of it that has either been killed (usually
through treatment with heat or chemicals) or has been attenuated
– weakened so that it can't cause the full disease. The part of the
pathogen that causes illness is separated from the part that prompts
an immune response. Supplying only the latter prompts the body to
make antibodies, but presents no risk of illness.

The idea that disease is caused by germs was originally only one of several theories. It was championed by Louis Pasteur and Robert Koch in the mid-19th century, and supported by their discoveries of bacteria that were responsible for particular diseases. Pasteur first discovered that microbes are responsible for fermentation and for food spoiling, and soon after discovered that they can be pathogens – things that cause disease. In 1881, he discovered the bacterium that causes pneumonia and meningitis; Robert Koch discovered that responsible for tuberculosis in 1882, and that for cholera in 1884; Edwin Klebs found the diphtheria bacterium in 1883. Pasteur also isolated the virus that causes rabies, too small to see with contemporary microscopes.

In the early 20th century, the search for vaccines to protect against some of the other terrible diseases that ravaged the population began. Among the first to be tackled was diphtheria, which can cause suffocation when membranes grow, blocking the throat. The first vaccine, developed in 1914, mixed the antitoxin given to affected patients with the diphtheria toxin itself to prompt immunity. A better vaccine was produced in 1923 and the terrible death rate of children from diphtheria fell dramatically. A vaccine for yellow fever followed in 1936. The triple vaccine for diphtheria, tetanus and pertussis (whooping cough) was introduced in 1942.

The triple vaccine against measles, mumps and rubella, MMR, was introduced in 1971. In 1978, measles was targeted for elimination and by 1981 cases had dropped. But then in 1998, Andrew Wakefield threw a spanner in the works with a fraudulent claim that the MMR vaccine could lead to autism in vaccinated children. Vaccination rates dropped to below the level needed to sustain herd immunity, allowing the diseases to spread again. Although most of Wakefield's collaborators renounced their results, all subsequent research has found no link and Wakefield has been banned from practicing medicine on the grounds of misconduct, some people still believe the false research. Vaccination rates have not fully recovered and measles is back.

Polio is a disease that attacks the nervous system, frequently leaving victims paralyzed and with wasted limbs. It became increasingly common in the U.S.A during the early decades of the 20th century, leading to annual fear as epidemics often raged during the summer months. These became worse and worse as the century went on.

The quest for a vaccine began in earnest in the 1930s, after the successful development of a vaccine against diphtheria in 1923. The first trials, in 1935, were disastrous, leading to many test subjects developing polio. Some died, many were paralyzed and some suffered an allergic reaction to the vaccine.

Two researchers working independently spearheaded the hunt for a vaccine: Jonas Salk and Albert Sabin. Salk produced his vaccine first and began trials of it early, spurred to urgent action by the worst summer epidemic in the U.S.A.'s history in 1952. Large-scale trials followed in 1954, funded by the March of Dimes and involving 1.3 million children. The vaccine proved effective and was licenced for use in 1955, to the jubilation of the American public. Salk's vaccine was made from polio virus that had been killed. Just a few weeks after mass vaccination began, some batches of incorrectly prepared vaccine caused cases of polio, resulting in 11 deaths and many cases of paralysis. Vaccination was suspended for a while, and the public lost confidence in it. Sabin continued to develop his oral vaccine, testing it extensively in the U.S.S.R. in 1959. It eventually overtook Salk's, being easier to administer, cheaper and more effective.

Though polio was the most feared disease of the 20th century, the defeat of other deadly diseases including diphtheria and pertussis (whooping cough) through vaccination were equally important triumphs of medical science.

—◦◦◇◦◦—

A Timeline: the Before, During and After of Polio Vaccinations

1796 Edward Jenner develops the first vaccine, to protect against smallpox.

1892 Antitoxin for diphtheria is developed (given after the disease is contracted).

1894 The first epidemic of polio in the U.S.

1923 A better diphtheria vaccine, diphtheria toxoid, is developed.

1935 Early trials of a polio vaccine are disastrous, with some patients dying or being paralyzed.

1936 Max Theiler develops a vaccine against yellow fever.

1938 Entertainer Eddie Cantor initiates the March of Dimes to raise money for research into polio.

1942 The DTP vaccine is introduced, a combined vaccine for diphtheria, tetanus and pertussis (whooping cough).

1952 A massive polio epidemic in the U.S.A leaves 21,000 people paralyzed.

1952 Jonas Salk begins early trials of his polio vaccine.

1954 Salk begins large-scale trials of his vaccine.

1955 Salk's vaccine is approved for use.

1959 Trials using Sabin's oral polio vaccine begin in the U.S.S.R..

1962 A measles vaccine is produced.

1971 The MMR triple vaccine is licenced.

1980 The WHO (World Health Organization) declares smallpox to have been eradicated.

1988 Polio is targeted for worldwide eradication.

1998 The safety of the MMR vaccine is challenged, but these concerns are later discredited.

IVF: THE FIRST TEST-TUBE BABY

1978

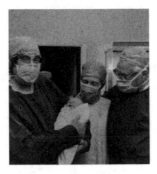

"The greatest of all curses is the curse of sterility."

Franklin D. Roosevelt, 1910.

Until the 18th century, people believed that all the important material for a baby was carried in the father's sperm, the mother providing only an environment in which the baby grows. The Italian biologist Lazzaro Spallanzani showed in 1780 that both egg and sperm are needed to create offspring, a result he found by carrying out artificial insemination in dogs. The earliest-known human artificial insemination by donor was unethical by any standards. The woman was under general anaesthetic and unaware of William Pancoast's plan. Her husband was infertile and the couple had been unable to conceive. Pancoast used donor sperm to inseminate the woman, who gave birth nine months later. Pancoast later told the woman's husband what he had done.

Early experiments in IVF met with popular and professional hostility, which made progress slow. In 1934, Gregory Pincus succeeded in fertilizing rabbit eggs *in vitro*, but when he reported his findings his work was criticized and Harvard refused to give him tenure. It was another ten years before John Rock and Miriam Menkin successfully fertilized a human egg *in vitro* after leaving the egg and sperm in contact for longer than usual. They made no attempt to implant the egg. Even so, in 1949 the Vatican denounced all IVF work.

The most important breakthrough came in 1951 with the discovery of sperm capacitation – chemical changes that take place in the sperm inside the woman's body before the egg is fertilized. This stage thins the membrane around the sperm, making it easier for it to fuse with an egg. Triggering capacitation by exposing the sperm to suitable chemicals and the right temperature made *in vitro* fertilization much more reliable. In 1961, Daniele Petrucci in Italy claimed to have grown a human embryo for 29 days, by which time it had developed a heartbeat. He then destroyed it. The following year, he claimed to have successfully implanted a fertilized egg in a patient, but this was never confirmed.

Since the first IVF birth of Louise Brown, more than a million babies have been born after *in vitro* fertilization. The technique has been used, sometimes controversially, to enable post-menopausal women to have babies, and, from 1985, with surrogate mothers who grow the child for genetic parents who are not able to go through a pregnancy. It is used alongside genetic testing, too, since it allows a batch of eggs to be fertilized, then any carrying a serious genetic condition to be rejected, implanting only healthy eggs back into the mother. IVF and artificial insemination have also both been used to help increase the numbers of endangered species.

IVF – *in vitro* fertilization – has brought joy to millions of parents since the first "test-tube baby" was born in 1978. The technique involves fertilizing a human egg cell outside the body and then implanting it to grow normally in the uterus. It was developed to help couples with infertility problems. It is now sometimes used to screen embryos for life-limiting or other serious genetic conditions if the parents are known to be carriers. IVF is also now used with other animals in farming, conservation work and reproductive research.

After the first successful *in vitro* fertilization of a human egg in 1969, it was nearly ten years before the first human IVF pregnancy. The technique was perfected in rabbits and hamsters and only attempted in humans once it was clear that the offspring developed normally to adulthood and had a normal lifespan for their species. Louise Brown was the first baby born after IVF treatment, on 25 July 1978, in Manchester, England. The process and pregnancy were overseen by Patrick Steptoe and Robert Edwards. They removed an egg through a tiny incision in the mother's abdomen. The egg was fertilized with the father's sperm in liquid that mimics conditions in the woman's body. After growing in a petri dish (*in vitro*) for two and a half days, the egg was returned to the mother's body for a normal pregnancy. The petri dish used for Louise Brown is still preserved in the Cambridge fertility clinic where her life began.

Steptoe and Edwards faced hostility and suspicion when they began to experiment with human IVF. The Medical Research Council in Britain refused them funding. They set up their project independently, and had no difficulty finding infertile couples happy to be part of their research – though participants were sworn to secrecy for their own protection. The process was a strain for parents, and had a success rate of only 12 percent in its early days. By 2013, 35 years after the birth of Louise Brown, five million babies had been born by IVF. The procedure has become far more streamlined and straightforward, and the success rate is now around 25 percent.

A Timeline: the Before, During and After of the First Test-tube Baby

1677 Antonie van Leeuwenhoek first looks at his sperm through a microscope.

1759 Caspar Wolff proposes that the different parts of a growing baby develop from different layers of cells, which we now know to be correct.

1780 Lazzaro Spallanzani carries out artificial insemination in dogs.

1827 It is discovered that women have ova (egg cells).

1855 J. Marion Sims tries artificial insemination, achieving one pregnancy from 55 attempts; it ends in miscarriage.

1875 Oscar Hertwig demonstrates that fertilization is the fusing of the nucleus of an egg cell with a sperm cell.

1884 In the U.S.A., William Pancoast uses artificial insemination by donor successfully.

1934 Gregory Pincus carries out IVF experiments on rabbits; he is denounced for his work and Harvard refuses him tenure.

1944 John Rock and Miriam Menkin achieve successful fertilization *in vitro* of a human egg.

1949 The Vatican denounces IVF.

1951 The discovery of sperm capacitation makes fertilization more reliable.

1968 Patrick Steptoe and Robert Edwards succeed in fertilizing human eggs *in vitro*.

1978 Louise Brown, the first baby to result from IVF, is born.

1985 The first successful pregnancy by surrogacy is achieved.

1995 The birth of the first "test-tube gorilla".

SCIENCE

Quantum Theory: Waves and Particles as One

Discovering the Structure of the Atom

Einstein and his Theories of Relativity

The Story of Humankind: Lucy Skeleton Discovery

Stephen Hawking, Black Holes
and Release of *A Brief History of Time*

Scientists Clone Dolly

QUANTUM THEORY: WAVES AND PARTICLES AS ONE

1900

"Experience will prove whether this hypothesis
is realized in nature."

Max Planck on the existence of energy quanta.

Two thousand years ago, the Roman philosopher Lucretius claimed that light is made of particles. Isaac Newton favored the particle theory, too, in 1704, but by the time Newton was writing, the wave theory promoted by Christiaan Huygens in 1679 was more popular. In 1800, Thomas Young shone light through an apparatus with two slits and found interference patterns on the far side. This supported the theory of light as waves. In the 1870s, James Clerk Maxwell showed visible light as part of the electromagnetic spectrum. The parts are distinguished by wavelength, so the nature of light seemed finally to have been determined.

In 1909, Geoffrey Taylor repeated Young's double-slit experiment, but firing only one photon at a time. There should be no interference pattern, as the photon must go through one slit or the other. Yet interference patterns did develop. Each photon appeared to split in half and go through both slits at the same time, then recombine into a single photon on the other side. When Taylor then put a photon detector at each slit, the pattern changed. Now the photons behaved only as particles. They seemed to "know" that there was a particle detector present. They behaved as waves when he was looking for waves and particles when he was looking for particles.

The more famous particle of energy is the electron, the first subatomic particle discovered. In 1909, Robert Millikan and Harvey Fletcher carried out an experiment in which they suspended a droplet of oil in an electric field, then let it fall and calculated the exact force needed to hold it in place against gravity. From this, they calculated the charge of an electron: 1.592×10^{-19} coulomb, the first measurable energy quantum. In 1923, Arthur Compton showed the quantum nature of X-rays. He showed that X-rays fired at a thin sheet of gold leaf bounce off with reduced energy (a larger wavelength), and the change in wavelength is always a fixed amount – a quantum.

Just as light can act as a particle or a wave, so can other subatomic particles. In 1924, Louis de Broglie calculated the wavelength of a photon, deriving an equation that could be used to calculate the wavelength of other particles, too. That other particles can actually behave as waves was demonstrated in 1927 by Clinton Davisson and Lester Germer. They fired electrons at a nickel crystal and saw diffraction as though the electrons were waves. As soon as we think of matter as waves, any kind of certainty about its position disappears. Indeed, the Uncertainty Principle, stated by Werner Heisenberg in 1927, says just this: we can either know one set of properties with certainty or another, but never both.

When the young Max Planck asked his professor Philipp von Jolly about the prospects of a career in physics, von Jolly advised him that physics was pretty much complete, with nothing left to discover. Fortunately, Planck ignored his advice. He went on to lay the foundations of quantum theory that, together with Einstein's theory of relativity, completely revolutionized physics – and has left us with plenty still to discover.

In 1900, Planck was investigating one of the few puzzles remaining in classical physics.

A black body does not emit electromagnetic radiation in the way that would be expected. In physics, a "black body" is an opaque, non-reflective object. If it is kept at a constant temperature, it emits electromagnetic radiation. The spectrum emitted depends on the temperature. Even though it looks black at room temperature, it is emitted infrared (which we can't see). As it heats up, it glows dull red, bright red through orange and eventually white. This so-called black-box radiation confounded all attempts to be shoehorned into the laws of physics. In what he later called an "act of desperation", Planck stopped treating light as a wave and tried using discrete chunks of energy of fixed amounts in his equations. These chunks he called "quanta" (singular, quantum). Suddenly, it all worked.

But everyone knew light was a wave – it had been known for centuries. Few people were enthusiastic about his suggestion (including Planck himself). Yet now, quanta of energy lie at the heart of physics and chemistry. They explain how chemicals react together, how electricity and electromagnetic radiation behave, and the structure of atoms.

———◇◇◇◇◇———

A Timeline: the Before, During and After of Quantum Theory

1679 Christiaan Huygens describes light as a wave of energy.

1704 Isaac Newton describes light as being made of "corpuscles" – tiny, weightless particles.

1900 Max Planck suggests that energy comes in discrete chunks, or "quanta".

1905 Albert Einstein proposes the existence of the photon as a quantum of light energy.

1909 Geoffrey Taylor's double-slit experiment shows that light can behave as particles or as waves.

1913 Robert Millikan calculates the charge of an electron as 1.592×10^{-19} coulomb.

1913 Niels Bohr suggests a structure for the atom that takes account of quantum ideas.

1923 Arthur Compton discovers the particle nature of X-rays, confirming quantum theory.

1924 Louis de Broglie proposes that matter has wave properties.

1925 Wolfgang Pauli proposes the Pauli Exclusion Principle that, in simple terms, says that two particles with physical extension cannot occupy the same space at the same time.

1926 Gilbert Lewis names the light quantum a "photon".

1927 The Davisson–Germer experiment confirms that electrons can behave as waves.

1927 Werner Heisenberg states the Uncertainty Principle – that we can't know both the precise momentum and the precise location of a particle at the same time.

DISCOVERING THE STRUCTURE OF THE ATOM

1911

"[It was] quite the most incredible event that has ever happened to me in my life. It was almost as incredible as if you fired a 15-inch shell at a piece of tissue paper and it came back and hit you."

Ernest Rutherford.

J. J. Thomson had discovered the electron in 1897, the first subatomic particle to be recognized. In 1904, he proposed a model of the atom in which a cloud or soup of positive charge is studded with charged "corpuscles" carrying a negative electrical charge. Others described this as a positively charged "pudding" dotted with negatively charged "raisins". The same year, the Japanese physicist Hantaro Nagaoka proposed a planetary model of atomic structure, with the atom surrounded by electrons orbiting in the manner of Saturn's rings. His predictions of a comparatively large nucleus and orbiting electrons were both correct, but the detail was wrong...

The Danish physicist Niels Bohr extended Ernest Rutherford's model of the atom in 1913, in line with quantum theory. In his model – which is still basically current – electrons orbit the nucleus in clearly defined "shells" or spaced orbits. The energy associated with particular orbits varies, but only in line with fixed quanta (parcels) of energy. If an electron jumps from one orbit to one with a lower energy, a quantum of energy is released. It is for this reason that atoms emit light in fixed wavelengths: a photon with a certain amount of energy is emitted as an electron moves between shells. Their being contained in shells also explains why they do not immediately fall towards the positive nucleus, a puzzle that Rutherford could not solve.

Although Bohr worked out that electrons release or absorb a quantum of energy when jumping between shells, he offered no explanation as to why this happens. That piece of the puzzle was found by Louis de Broglie in 1924. De Broglie suggested that any particle had an associated wavelength, calculated by dividing Planck's constant by the momentum of the particle. When an electron drops to a lower atomic orbit (closer to the nucleus), its frequency changes, and the extra energy is disposed of by emitting a photon. When Louis de Broglie won the 1929 Nobel Prize in Physics for his work, it was the first time the prize had been awarded for a PhD thesis.

After discovering the atomic nucleus in 1911, Rutherford assumed that it was made of a positively charged particle which balanced the negative charge on the electron. In 1917, he demonstrated that firing alpha particles (helium nuclei) at nitrogen produced hydrogen nuclei. (This was the first nuclear reaction.) Neither experiment nor theory were consistent with the nucleus containing only a single type of particle, though, so, in 1920, he suggested that the nucleus consisted of positively charged protons and some type of neutral particle. It was James Chadwick, examining a new type of radiation, who discovered the neutron in 1932 – an uncharged particle of about the same mass as the proton.

The now-familiar model of the atom that has a nucleus orbited by electrons originated with the New Zealand-born physicist Ernest Rutherford in 1911. During one of his many experiments on radioactivity, he directed Ernest Marsden and Hans Geiger firing a beam of alpha particles (helium nuclei) at a very thin sheet of gold foil. As they expected, most passed straight through – but a few bounced off.

This result was stunning, and forced Rutherford to reconsider the structure of the atom as it was then conceived. Instead of the atom being of fairly uniform construction, Rutherford proposed that the vast majority of its mass is concentrated into a very dense but tiny nucleus and most of the rest of it is empty space, with electrons orbiting the nucleus at a considerable distance. The few alpha particles that had bounced back had collided with and been repelled by a positively charged nucleus. He calculated that the nucleus represents only about about 1/10,000th of the radius of the atom. This was an astonishing discovery. It means that, if the nucleus were a beach ball 40cm (16in) wide, the outer electron would be 4km (2.5 miles) away.

Rutherford's nuclear model of atomic structure was revolutionary in more ways than one, as it introduced the idea that atoms have parts – that there are subatomic particles. He went on to isolate the proton in 1920 and propose the existence of the neutron, the other particle in the nucleus. The electron had already been discovered by J.J. Thomson in 1897.

—∞∞∞∞—

A Timeline: the Before, During and After of the Discovery of the Structure of the Atom

1815 William Prout suggests that all atoms are made up of combined hydrogen atoms.

1894 G.J. Stoney proposes the name "electron" for "atoms of electricity".

1897 J.J. Thomson discovers the electron.

1904 J.J. Thomson proposes the "plum pudding" model of the atom.

1904 Hantaro Nagaoka describes the planetary model, with a large nucleus surrounded by electrons orbiting in rings in the same plane.

1905 Albert Einstein's paper on Brownian motion suggests a proof that atoms and molecules exist.

1911 Jean Perrin provides experimental proof of the existence of atoms, following Einstein's lead.

1911 Ernest Rutherford publishes his account of the structure of the atom.

1919 Rutherford reports his discovery of the proton.

1920 Rutherford and William Draper Harkins both independently propose the existence of a neutral atomic particle, the neutron.

1932 James Chadwick discovers the neutron.

EINSTEIN AND HIS THEORIES OF RELATIVITY

1915

"It has become appallingly obvious that our technology has exceeded our humanity."

Albert Einstein.

Albert Einstein was no child prodigy. He was slow to talk and failed the entrance exam for university. After graduating from the polytechnic in Zurich, Switzerland, he could not find teaching work and took a job in the Patent Office. He pursued his interest in physics in the evenings, and gained his PhD in 1905. The General Theory of Relativity established his global reputation. He settled in the U.S. in 1935 to escape persecution by the Nazis, becoming an American citizen in 1940. Despite being a pacifist, he worked on the Manhattan Project to develop nuclear weapons, as he feared Germany would develop the bomb first. He spent his last years seeking an elusive unifying theory that would bind all physics together.

Einstein's paper on the movement of atoms explained Brownian motion – the movement of pollen particles in water observed by Robert Brown in 1827. Einstein explained that the pollen is jostled by molecules of water. This was definitive proof of the existence of atoms and molecules, previously proposed but not demonstrated.

Einstein's final paper of 1905 was on the equivalence of energy and mass. It contains the first version of his famous equation, $E=mc^2$. The fact that matter can be converted to energy makes nuclear power and nuclear weapons possible.

The four papers of his *annus mirabilis* made Einstein's name. The first, on the photoelectric effect, used Max Planck's theory of quanta, or discrete packets of energy that cannot be divided. Einstein's explanation of the photoelectric effect relied on light quanta-displacing electrons (which we can think of as electricity quanta) and so producing an electric current. The idea that light is formed of quanta met considerable resistance until Robert Millikan proved it in 1919. The photoelectric effect is exploited in solar power cells, which convert the light energy of the sun into electricity by this means.

The proof of Einstein's General Theory of Relativity came in 1919. Einstein had proposed in 1911 that during an eclipse, a star behind the sun should be visible, its light skirting around the sun, bent by the sun's gravity. Normally, the sun is too bright for the effect to be visible, but when it is darkened by a total eclipse that obstacle is removed. Arthur Eddington, Cambridge professor of astronomy, sailed to Principe off the coast of Africa to photograph the eclipse. Despite cloudy weather for the first 400 seconds, he took a conclusive photograph in the last ten seconds: Einstein's account of gravity is closer to reality than Newton's.

Albert Einstein (1879–1955) must be the most famous scientist of the 20th century, though very few people understood his ideas when he first stated them.

Einstein felt that Newtonian physics had limitations when applied to new developments, and set out to correct this. His great breakthrough came in 1905, his *annus mirabilis* ("miraculous year"). He published four groundbreaking papers – on the photoelectric effect, the movement of atoms, special relativity and the equivalence of energy and mass. Together, these moved physics into a new era.

His theory of special relativity demonstrated that the speed of light is absolute – it is the same regardless of the position of the observer – but that time and space are relative, changing with the conditions of the observer. Traveling at great speed (near the speed of light) makes time pass more slowly.

Einstein was aware that the theory did not take account of gravity. He spent the next ten years wrestling with the very complex math he needed to make it generally applicable throughout the universe. Finally, in 1916, he published the theory of general relativity. In it, he explains gravity as a distortion of the space–time continuum caused by the presence of massive objects. A massive star bends space and time, rather like a heavy ball makes a dip in a blanket pulled taut. The effect is that other bodies of lesser mass "fall" towards the heavier mass.

————∞∞∞∞————

A Timeline: the Life, Experience and Influence of the Albert Einstein

1827 Robert Brown reports the random movements of pollen grains in water, now known as Brownian motion.

March 14, 1879 Albert Einstein is born in Ulm Württemberg, Germany.

1902 Unable to find any work as a teacher or academic, Albert Einstein takes a job as a clerk at the Swiss Patent Office.

1905 In this annus mirabilis – miraculous year – Albert Einstein publishes four major theoretical papers, including the first published exploration of the Theory of Special Relativity and the first formulation of the famous equation E=mc2.

1915 Einstein completes his general theory of relativity.

May 29, 1919 A solar eclipse provides dramatic observable evidence that Einstein's General Theory of Relativity is correct.

1921 Albert Einstein wins the Nobel Prize in Physics for his work on the photoelectric effect, first published in 1905.

1922 Key publication of Alezander Friedmann's equations proposing an expanding Universe.

1924 Edwin Hubble proves there are galaxies outside the Milky Way, the first step towards proof of the big bang theory and the theory of general relativity.

1932 The Kennedy–Thorndike experiment provides proof that the speed of light is, in fact, constant.

April 18, 1955 Einstein dies in Princeton Hospital at the age of 76.

1959 Time dilation, predicted by Einstein in 1908, is demonstrated: time passes very slightly more slowly at the bottom of a mountain than at the top, as gravity effectively slows it down.

THE STORY OF HUMANKIND: LUCY SKELETON DISCOVERY

1974

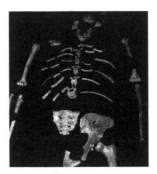

"In our case, finding a Lucy is unique. No one will ever find another Lucy. You can't order one from a biological supply house. It's a unique discovery, a unique specimen."

Donald Johanson.

When Charles Darwin published *On the Origin of Species by Means of Natural Selection* in 1859, it was immediately contentious. Darwin was suggesting that nature changes over time, and that humans, too, could have changed over time. It was taken by many as an affront to the Biblical account of Earth's history. In some places, that view is still widely held. For other people, it suggested new avenues for science to explore. One of those people was Eugène Dubois, who went first to Sumatra and then to Java to hunt for an early human ancestor. In 1891, he found one: the first early hominid discovered, *Homo erectus*, who lived around a million years ago.

When the Taung Child was found in Taung, South Africa in 1924, it was first dismissed as an unimportant ape. It took many years for the importance of this, the first instance of *Australopithecus afarensis*, to be recognized. Instead, attention focused on Peking Man, found in China in 1927, which was consistent with the belief that humans evolved in Asia or Europe. We now know that *Homo erectus* evolved from *Homo ergaster*, who migrated from Africa around 1.8 million years ago. *Homo ergaster* was discovered in 1949, but not identified until 1975. Africa was finally confirmed as the cradle of humanity in 1960 when *Homo habilis* was found in Africa. At 1.75 million years old, it was older than any *Homo* species then recognized.

Despite the research linking modern humans with earlier hominids, and the ongoing search for a common ancestor who marked the point at which our evolution parted company with that of chimpanzees, few people really thought of humans as animals like any others. Their complacency was challenged by a book called *The Naked Ape*, published by Desmond Morris in 1967. Morris was the keeper of mammals at London Zoo and presented humans for the first time in the same way as other mammals are studied – with descriptions of habit, mating behavior, rearing of young, fighting and so on. Humanity's specialness was stripped away completely.

At the time of Lucy's discovery, only around eight human ancestors were known; around 20 are now identified. It is no longer assumed that there was a direct line of descent from a common human/chimpanzee ancestor to modern humans. There might have been dead ends, with early human species dying off or breeding with others and not necessarily leading to modern humans in a straight line. In 2001 and 2002, the discovery of Toumai, *Sahelanthropus tchadensis*, in North Africa added further complications. At 6–7 million years old, Tumai could be a common ancestor of chimpanzees and humans – or be related to both but an ancestor of neither.

❧

On November 24, 1974, Donald Johanson and Maurice Taieb made an astonishing discovery in a ditch in Ethiopia. They recognized immediately that the bones they had found belonged to an early human ancestor. These turned out to fragments of a skeleton of *Australopithecus afarensis*, and the most important proto-human remains ever found.

The skeleton, later named Lucy, is 3.2 million years old, pushing early human evolution back by 400,000 years and siting it in Africa. The discovery of Lucy was particularly exciting because 40 percent of her bones were recovered, including parts of the ribs and skull, which rarely survive. Lucy spent most of her time walking upright, a distinctive characteristic of humans, and is the earliest we know to have done so. She might also have spent time in the trees; she had long, trailing arms like a baboon. Her teeth are between those found in other apes and human teeth; her brain was smaller than a human brain. For a while, it looked as if Lucy might represent the most recent common ancestor of both humans and chimpanzees.

An example of *A. afarensis* had been found in 1924, the Taung Child, but was dismissed as an ape of no significance. By the time Lucy was discovered, the importance of *A. afarensis* was recognized. Although older and more complete fossils of *A. afarensis* have been found since, Lucy sparked a new era of investigation into human ancestry.

———◦○◇○◦———

A Timeline: the Before, During and After of the Discovery of "Lucy"

1891 *Homo erectus* (in the form of Java Man) is discovered by Eugène Dubois.

1912 The fossil remains of what was claimed as an early human are discovered in Piltdown, UK, and named the Piltdown Man.

1924 Taung Child is discovered in South Africa, the first specimen of *Australopithecus afarensis,* but his importance is disputed.

1927 A collection of bones is found in a cave in China, later named Peking Man.

1949 Remains of *Homo ergaster* are discovered in Africa, the earliest known human species, but they are not recognized as such at the time.

1953 Piltdown Man is revealed as a fake, made of parts less than 50,000 years old.

1960 In Africa, Jonathan Leakey discovers fossil remains of *Homo habilis*, a new species of man and the earliest traced to Africa.

1967 *The Naked Ape*, by Desmond Morris is published.

1974 The remains of Lucy are discovered in East Africa.

1975 *Homo ergaster* is identified in southern Africa.

2001–2 The discovery of the *Sahelanthropus tchadensis* in Chad complicates the evolutionary relationship between humans and chimpanzees.

2004 *Homo floresiensis* is discovered, a very short human species only 1m (3ft) tall and so nicknamed "Hobbit".

2015 A new species of *Homo* ancestor, *Australopithecus deyiremeda,* is found in Chad, thought to have lived alongside Lucy and two other species.

STEPHEN HAWKING, BLACK HOLES AND RELEASE OF *A BRIEF HISTORY OF TIME*

1988

"We are each free to believe what we want and it is my view that the simplest explanation is there is no God. No one created the universe and no one directs our fate. This leads me to a profound realization. There is probably no heaven, and no afterlife either. We have this one life to appreciate the grand design of the universe, and for that, I am extremely grateful."

Stephen Hawking.

The phenomena later known as black holes were first predicted in 1916 by Karl Schwarzchild. When a star at least three times the mass of the sun dies, it leaves behind a core that collapses in on itself under its own gravity. It becomes super dense – such a star would occupy a sphere about the radius of New York city. A black hole grows by drawing in other matter. It can be very destructive, ripping matter away from passing stars or engulfing entire planets or stars. The new matter is also hugely compressed. At the centre of a black hole is a "singularity" where density and gravity are infinite.

The common view of a black hole is that nothing can escape its extremely powerful gravitational pull. Hawking proposed in 1974 that at the very edge of a black hole – the event horizon, the point where that pull becomes irresistible – particle–anti-particle pairs are created. Their creation uses energy from the black hole's gravity. One of the pair is sucked into the black hole and the other escapes. It should be observed as black-body radiation. The particle that has escaped was produced using energy from the black hole and so represents a net loss of energy (and so mass) to the black hole. If a black hole is not increasing in mass by drawing in other matter, it will slowly shrink and eventually evaporate in this way.

In 1981, Hawking suggested that there might be no boundary to the universe – meaning that there was no beginning or end to it as well as no edge to it in space. This makes "before the Big Bang" a meaningless concept; time did not exist before the Big Bang. This is rather like saying that if you stand at the North Pole, the concept "north" has no meaning as there is nowhere further north to go. Hawking has also suggested that the universe could have many histories, which add together to give its present state. In his model, the traditional singularity from which the universe erupted is replaced with something more like the North Pole.

Hawking is pessimistic about the prospects for humanity. He has several times voiced his opinion that humankind is set on a course of self-destruction, whether through war, climate change, the release of a genetically engineered virus or some other means. He has suggested that although the development of artificial intelligence is possible, it should be avoided: the outcome of creating beings that will become more intelligent than ourselves is very uncertain, and it could be both the biggest and last event in human history. He has promoted space exploration, believing that we might need to expand to other planets in order to survive. He says that it is highly likely that aliens exist, but that trying to contact them would be inadvisable.

Stephen Hawking is surely the most famous living physicist. Diagnosed with the degenerative neural condition motor neurone disease (MND) at the age of just 21, his entire career has been conducted in the grip of increasing disability.

As a research student at Cambridge, Hawking became interested in the work of Roger Penrose on the origins of the universe, the fate of stars and the creation of black holes. Hawking's own work came to focus on black holes. The discovery that made him famous within the scientific community came in 1974, when he revealed that black holes are not quite as all-consuming as they seem. In fact, he said, radiation should be able to escape from the edge of a black hole. This hypothetical radiation became known as Hawking radiation. It provides a way for small black holes (smaller than the mass of the moon) to shrink and eventually evaporate.

Hawking became famous outside scientific circles with the publication of *A Brief History of Time* in 1988. This book tries to explain 20th-century cosmological theory in a form that lay readers can understand. A later version, *A Briefer History of Time*, was easier to understand.

In 2014, the award-winning film *The Theory of Everything* popularized Hawking's story and sparked a fresh wave of public interest in his works and his life.

———oo◇oo———

A Timeline: the Life, Experience and Influence of the Stephen Hawking

1915 Albert Einstein publishes the general theory of relativity.

1915 Karl Schwarzchild uses Einstein's generaltheory of relativity to describe black holes and defines their gravitational radius (Schwarzschild radius).

1931 Georges Lemaître publishes his theory that the universe began from a singularity, later called the Big Bang theory.

1942 Stephen Hawking is born in Oxford, England.

1963 Hawking is diagnosed with motor neurone disease (MND).

1963 The term "black hole" is first used at the Texas Symposium on Relativistic Astrophysics.

1973 With co-author George Ellis, Hawking publishes *The Large Scale Structure of Space-Time* that explains the foundations of space-time and its infinite expansion.

1985 Hawking loses his voice to a tracheotomy operation and receives an electronic voice synthesizer.

1988 *A Brief History of Time* is published, the popular account of his work in cosmology.

2007 Hawking experiences zero-gravity in a modified jumbo jet during a visit to the Kennedy Space Center.

SCIENTISTS CLONE DOLLY

1997

"Dolly is derived from a mammary gland cell and we couldn't think of a more impressive pair of glands than Dolly Parton's."

Dr Ian Wilmut explains the rationale behind
the name of the sheep clone, Dolly.

In 1952, American scientists Robert Briggs and Thomas King successfully cloned the first frog. To create the frog, the scientists used the same nuclear transfer technique that would be employed 44 years later to clone Dolly the Sheep. This meant transferring the nucleus – or genetic material – from an early tadpole embryo into a frog egg that had had the nucleus removed. The resulting cell then grew into a tadpole. The experiment was an important breakthrough, because it showed that "nuclear transfer" was a viable cloning technique. It also indicated that early embryonic cells are better for cloning than cells at later stages. Briggs and King found that those tadpoles cloned from more advanced embryos tended to grow into frogs with abnormalities. In 1975, British scientist J. Derek Bromhall used a tiny glass straw to transfer the nucleus from a rabbit embryo into a rabbit egg cell without a nucleus. This method of transfer was necessary because mammalian egg cells are much smaller than those of frogs, so are harder to manipulate.

Bromhall considered the experiment a success when a rabbit embryo began to develop a few days later. However, Bromhall did not carry his work to its conclusion by implanting the embryo into a rabbit mother's womb.

Danish scientist Steen Willadsen became the first person to successfully clone a mammal in 1984, when he used cells from early embryos to clone sheep. Willadsen did this by separating one cell from an eight-cell lamb embryo and fusing it into an egg cell without a nucleus. The resulting embryos were implanted into a surrogate mother sheep who went on to give birth to three lambs. Willadsen's experiment showed that a mammal could be cloned by nuclear transfer, even though the donor nuclei in this case came from early embryonic cells. Dr Ian Wilmut would take this one step further 13 years later by cloning a sheep from adult cells.

In 1997, a team of U.S. scientists led by Dr Gerald Schatten became the first to clone a primate, the closest animal relative to humans. Schatten's team used a different method to the one used to clone Dolly the Sheep. Instead of transferring a nucleus into an empty egg cell, the scientists split the original cells in an embryo to make identical animals. The result was the cloning of two baby rhesus monkeys, a female called Neti and a male called Ditto. The cloning of the monkeys was seen as a groundbreaking moment. As monkeys have such similar DNA to humans, scientists hope that monkey clones can be used for the study of human ailments. They could also be harvested for stem cells, the master cells that can develop into any type of cell in the body.

At the beginning of the 20th century, artificially creating life was a concept only explored by science fiction and gothic literature. However, by the end of the century, humans had found a way of cloning mammals. An example of this new scientific sensation was unveiled in 1997 in the form of Dolly the Sheep. Dolly was different from the various other organisms that had been cloned in the years leading up to her birth on July 5 1996, because she had been successfully cloned from an adult cell instead of from an embryo cell.

To create Dolly, a mammary gland cell was taken from one ewe and fused with a second ewe's unfertilized egg cell, which had had its nucleus removed. When the egg cell developed into an embryo it was transplanted into a surrogate mother, which then carried out a normal pregnancy and gave birth to Dolly. Dolly's birth was greeted with a frenzy of amazement, controversy and speculation about the future of cloning. For many, animal cloning raised ethical questions about how far humans should be allowed to interfere with the creation of life. Many feared that the birth of Dolly meant that human cloning was just around the corner.

In the U.S., President Bill Clinton ordered that a task force be set up to explore the legal and ethical implications of cloning. Clinton's successor, George W. Bush, made it known that he was repelled by the idea of human cloning, even for use in medical research. Dr Ian Wilmut himself, the Scottish scientist behind Dolly's birth, described human cloning as "repugnant". Many scientists in Japan and the U.S. felt vindicated in their views that cloned animals have short lifespans when Dolly was put to sleep at six-and-a-half years old after suffering from a progressive lung disease. Despite this, Dolly gave birth to six healthy lambs during her short lifetime.

———⬦⬦⬦———

A Timeline: the Life, Experience and Influence of Dolly

1938 Cloning is first envisioned by German Dr Hans Spemann, who proposes a form of nuclear transfer in cells.

1953 The structure of DNA (deoxyribonucleic acid) is discovered by Francis C. Crick and James D. Watson.

1973 Paul Berg and Stanley N. Cohen successfully splice a gene for the first time.

1978 The first child, Louise Brown, is conceived by *in vitro* fertilization (IVF).

1984 Danish Dr Steen Willadsen clones a lamb.

1993 The first human embryos are cloned in America. Cells taken from defective human embryos are grown *in vitro* and then destroyed at the 32-cell stage.

1994 American Dr Ned First clones calves from the cells of early embryos.

1995 Dr Ian Wilmut creates the world's first cloned sheep, Megan and Morag, from embryo cells at the Roslin Institute in Edinburgh, Scotland.

1996 Dr Ian Wilmut and his team clone Dolly, the world's first sheep created from adult cells.

1997 Two rhesus monkeys, Neti and Ditto, are cloned at the Oregon Regional Primate Research Center.

1997 Dr Ian Wilmut creates the first sheep with a human gene in every cell of its body, called Polly.

1999 Dr Gerald Schatten becomes the first person to use embryo splitting to create Tetra, a rhesus monkey.

1999 Dr Xiangzhong Yang successfully clones calves from frozen cells taken from a bull.

2000 The first patents for cloning are given to the scientists who cloned Dolly.

2000 Japanese scientists clone a young bull from a bull that was a clone itself, the first case of re-cloning with a large mammal.

2004 The first commercially produced pet, a cat called Little Nicky, is cloned.

2013 Dr Shoukhrat Mitalipov becomes the first person to use cell nuclear transfer to create a human embryo as a source of embryonic stem cells.

SPACE
AND THE
ENVIRONMENT

FIRST ROCKET INTO SPACE

1942

"It is difficult to say what is impossible, for the dream of yesterday is the hope of today and the reality of tomorrow."

Robert H. Goddard.

The principle of rocketry is very old. The Chinese were making rockets as fireworks and weapons hundreds of years ago; the use of fire arrows is first reported in 904ad during the siege of Yuzhang. A rocket works by explosively igniting fuel to create gases under high pressure that are pushed out of the back of the missile. This provides thrust, pushing the missile forwards. The fire arrow was propelled by a bag of gunpowder attached to the shaft. But the idea of a rocket powerful enough to go into space, or to propel a weapon a very long way, belongs firmly in the 20th century.

The first person to calculate that a rocket could be sent into space, and to write seriously about space travel, was the Russian scientist and philosopher Konstantin Tsiolkovsky in 1903. His work was little known in Europe and resulted in no practical developments. The American Robert Goddard launched a small, liquid-fuel powered rocket in 1926. It flew for only two-and-a-half seconds, reaching an altitude of just 12.5m (41ft) and landing 56m (184ft) away in a cabbage patch. Even so, it proved the concept of a rocket powered by burning liquid oxygen. He had said as early as 1920 that he could conceive of a rocket reaching the moon, though few others took this vision seriously.

The U.S.S.R.'s greatest proponent of space travel, Tsiolkovsky, was a mathematics teacher by day who wrote about and investigated rocketry in his spare time. In the West, lots of small groups of enthusiasts sprang up in Germany and elsewhere after Hermann Oberth published *The Rocket into Planetary Space*, a book on space travel in 1923. There was no official funding for research into rocketry or space travel until it became clear that rockets could be used to carry bombs.

It was from this group of enthusiasts that von Braun and the A4 emerged. When his rocket was perfected, it was not for his original purpose of space exploration, but as a weapon – Nazi funding was available for war but not for space.

V-2 rockets traveled faster than the speed of sound, taking only five seconds from launch in the Netherlands to hit London. They arrived silently, the noise of them whooshing through the air being audible only after they had hit their target. In later days, when the rockets to come out of von Braun's department at NASA began to carry payloads into space, the rockets would stream silently ahead of their own sounds, traveling at speeds of nearly 10,000kph (6,214mph), or nine times the speed of sound.

The launch of the first rocket that entered space – defined at the time as 80km (49 miles) above sea level – came in 1942 as part of the German development of rocketry for carrying bombs.

Wernher von Braun had hopes of making a rocket for space travel, and as a younger engineer joined an amateur rocketry club, Verein für Raumschiffarht (VfR) or Society for Space Travel. But it was the 1930s and the Nazis were looking for new weapons they could develop. The VfR was awarded $400 to develop a rocket. Von Braun's first rocket, the A4, was renamed the V-2 and used to deliver bombs. As the A4 made the transition to a weapon, development moved out of Berlin on to an island on the Baltic coast of Germany, Usedom. Here, secrecy was more easily preserved and there was more space for testing. The first test crashed into the sea, the second exploded at an altitude of 11km (7 miles), and the third flew to 80km (50 miles) and landed on target 193km (120 miles) away.

After the war, the U.S.A. was keen to appropriate German scientific expertise and took in many scientists who might otherwise have gone to the U.S.S.R.. Von Braun surrendered to the US with his 500-strong rocketry development team. To begin with, the impetus of rocketry development was still weaponry. But in 1958, NASA was formed in response to the Soviet launch of the satellite Sputnik, and interest turned towards space again – this time in a frenzied rush. Von Braun was invited to NASA in 1960 and became director of the Marshall Space Flight Center, where he directed the Saturn V launch and worked towards rockets later used in the moon landings.

The principle of the rocket, expelling exhaust gases at very high pressure from the rear to propel the rocket forward, relies on burning a large amount of fuel very quickly. A limiting factor is how much fuel can be packed into the rocket and – when it is in space – supplying oxygen to allow it to burn. Multi-stage rockets have extra fuel-carrying stages.

A Timeline: the Before, During and After of the First Rocket into Space

1903 Konstantin Tsiolkovsky publishes a book that includes the calculations to send a rocket into space.

1914 Robert Goddard registers two patents for rockets – one for a rocket using liquid fuel and one for a two- or three-stage rocket using solid fuel.

1920 Goddard's suggestion that a rocket might reach the moon is ridiculed in the American press.

1923 Hermann Oberth publishes a book about rocket flight into outer space.

1924 The Society for Studies of Interplanetary Travel is formed in the U.S.S.R., rooted in Tsiolkovsky's work.

1937 Oberth, Wernher von Braun and others form the Society for Space Travel in Germany, and go on to design the A4 rocket.

1942 The first V-2 rocket flies; the fourth one becomes the first object to be launched into space.

1944 The first deployment of the V-2 rocket in bombing raids occurs.

1950 The American rocket Bumper 2 is launched from Cape Canaveral, reaching a record altitude of 400km (244 miles).

1957 A Soviet R-7 rocket is used to launch Sputnik, the first-ever satellite.

1958 NASA is founded; von Braun is employed to develop rocketry.

SPUTNIK: FIRST STRIKE IN THE SPACE RACE

1957

"The new socialist society turns even the most daring of man's dreams into a reality."

TASS statement, October 4, 1957.

The first U.S. satellite, Explorer, was launched a few months after Sputnik, on January 31 1958. By then, the U.S.S.R. had already launched a second satellite, Sputnik 2, carrying the dog Laika into space. The Soviet space programme remained well ahead of NASA in the space race through the 1950s and the early 1960s. The U.S.S.R. achieved the first man in space, the first woman in space, the first space walk, the first spacecraft to impact the moon, the first craft to impact Venus, the first craft to orbit the moon and the first craft to achieve a soft landing on the moon. It was the U.S.A., though, who achieved the ultimate goal of landing astronauts on the moon in 1969.

Sputnik was designed to gather data about the upper atmosphere, and collecting atmospheric and weather-related data remains a task carried out by satellites. The first communications satellite, launched by the U.S.A. in 1960, was a giant silvered balloon, Echo 1, sometimes scathingly referred to as a satelloon. It provided a reflective surface from which radio signals could be bounced. Far from elegant, this solution had the disadvantage that there was rather random scattering, and it was a pretty hit-and-miss affair – but it set the telecommunications ball rolling (through space) and telecoms is now a major function of satellites.

Some satellites are now helping us learn about deep space. One of the most famous is the Hubble Space Telescope, launched in 1990, a high-resolution optical telescope in low-Earth orbit (600km/372 miles above the Earth). It has taken the clearest photographs we have of distant galaxies, as being outside the atmosphere spares it from interference and background light. But it's not just for pretty pictures: Hubble has provided the data needed to calculate the rate of expansion of the universe. It is the only space telescope that is managed and repaired by astronauts who work from another type of satellite – space stations.

Another of the now-ubiquitous uses of satellites is GPS (Global Positioning System). The algorithms used for GPS are simple: a position on Earth is triangulated with reference to three satellites of known location. The technique was developed the other way round, by two physicists trying to plot the path Sputnik had taken from changes in its radio signal. Their algorithms were reversed, years later, to locate a point on Earth from known satellite positions. At first, GPS was used only for military purposes, but after a Korean airliner was shot down in 1983 after accidentally straying into Soviet airspace, it was opened up for civilian use. A fully functional system with 24 satellites covering the whole surface of the globe became operational in 1995.

❦

The space race began when the Americans weren't looking; the first lap was won by the U.S.S.R. on October 4, 1957 with the surprise launch of Sputnik, the first satellite, into orbit around the Earth. In fact, both superpowers had been aiming to launch a satellite since the mid-1950s, but the American effort was still several months away from launch. Their satellite was also much smaller, at around 7kg (15lb), than Sputnik's 83.5kg (184lb). Sputnik orbited at 900km (558 miles) above Earth, taking around 96 minutes to complete its elliptical orbit at a speed of almost 30,000kph (18,640mph).

Sputnik was designed to collect data on the upper atmosphere. Despite the entirely benign, scientific target (in this instance), many people in the U.S.A. were alarmed by the apparent supremacy of the U.S.S.R. and feared that they could use a satellite to launch a nuclear weapon – it was the middle of the Cold War. Fear and humiliation spurred the U.S. to urgent action, with the rapid formation of NASA and launch of their own satellite – though not the satellite that had been scheduled for launch. That now looked rather paltry beside Sputnik. The new satellite, Explorer, was hurriedly put together, and a rocket adapted to carry it in just 84 days. Explorer remained in orbit until 1970, re-entering the atmosphere over the Pacific Ocean on March 31 after more than 58,000 orbits. An identically constructed flight backup of Explorer is on display in the Smithsonian Institution's National Air and Space Museum in Washington, DC.

———◦◦◦◦◦◦———

A Timeline: the Before, During and After of Sputnik

1951 The U.S.S.R. sends two dogs into space on a suborbital flight.

1952 The International Council of Scientific Unions (ICSU) names 1957–8 International Geophysical Year.

1954 The ICSU calls for satellites to be launched in 1957 to map the surface of the Earth.

1957 Sputnik, the first artificial satellite, is launched by the U.S.S.R..

1957 Sputnik 2, carrying the dog Laika, is launched.

1958 NASA is founded to spearhead the U.S.'s space mission; the Explorer satellite is launched.

1960 The U.S.A. launches the first communications satellite, Echo 1.

1971 The U.S.S.R. launches the first space station, Salyut 1.

1983 Korean airliner flight KAL 007 is shot down over the U.S.S.R., prompting the U.S. president Ronald Reagan to demand GPS is extended to civilian uses.

1986 The U.S.S.R. launches the first part of *Mir*, the first space station constructed in orbit from modules.

1989 The first fully functional GPS satellites are launched from the U.S.A.

1990 The Hubble Space Telescope is launched by NASA and ESA (the European Space Agency).

1995 The NAVSTAR GPS progamme, with 24 satellites, is fully operational.

2000 Full-resolution GPS is made available to the public, previously restricted to a deliberately degraded system, with the best data available only to the military.

CLIMATE CHANGE LABELLED A SERIOUS THREAT

1967

"At the moment we cannot predict what the overall climatic results will be of our using the atmosphere as a garbage dump."

Paul R. Ehrlich, *The Population Bomb*, 1968.

A link between atmospheric CO_2 and climate change was first proposed by Svante Arrhenuis in 1896. He set out to study the cause of the ice ages, and focused on the effects of CO_2 and water vapor trapping heat near the Earth's surface and acting like a greenhouse. Working before the age of computers, he carried out tens of thousands of calculations to reach his conclusion that halving the level of CO_2 would cause a temperature drop of 4–5°C, and doubling it would cause a rise of 5–6°C. From coal consumption at the time, he estimated that it would take 3,000 years to increase CO_2 by 50 percent and would bring pleasant,mild conditions.

From 1958 to 1960, Charles Keeling made crucial measurements at the Mauna Lao Observatory on Hawaii. He found that atmospheric CO_2 follows a seasonal pattern, rising in the northern hemisphere's winter and falling in the summer, but also showing an overall rise over the years. The seasonal pattern is accounted for by use of fossil fuels rising in the winter (for heating) and the uptake of CO_2 by plants being lower. In spring, uptake by plants begins to rise, and the level of CO_2 begins to fall. More important was the trend of an overall rise. Levels of CO_2 have now been mapped continuously since the start of Keeling's study and show a steady and accelerating rise, year on year.

There were plenty of dissenters in the early years. At first, people said the oceans would easily absorb any additional CO_2. Then there was the timescale – early models suggested that any rise in temperature would be very gradual, taking centuries. There were also plenty of people, both scientists and others, who thought that the warming seen over the previous century could have another cause, such as solar activity. Evidence from ice cores, which trap bubbles of air for hundreds of thousands of years, enabled scientists in the 1980s to analyze the atmosphere of the past. In 1978, it emerged that the level of CO_2 in the atmosphere was unprecedented, and steadily rising.

By the end of the 1980s, most scientists were convinced that there is a real problem. The Earth Summit in Rio de Janeiro, Brazil, in 1992, brought together representatives of 172 governments to tackle the problems of damage to the environment and climate change. It laid the groundwork for the Kyoto Protocol, which, in 1997, set out requirements for countries to limit carbon emissions. The target was to reduce greenhouse gas emissions to 5.2 per cent below their 1990 levels by 2012 in the developed countries. No country has achieved that target; CO_2 levels continue to climb and are now over 400ppm (parts per million).

The idea that gases such as carbon dioxide (CO_2), water vapor and methane might produce a greenhouse effect on Earth was first suggested in 1896. It only came to be considered a serious threat from 1967, though. In that year, the Japanese climatologist Syukuro Manabe used computers and a more complex model to re-examine the link between rising temperatures and the concentration of carbon dioxide in the atmosphere. His first trials found that doubling the CO_2 in the atmosphere would cause a rise of only 2°C. Manabe revised his model to take account of the potential of the oceans to act as a heat sink, deriving the first global ocean-coupled, climate-modelling program. The calculations were so complex that, using a computer with only 500Kb of memory, it took 50 days to run the program and return the results.

Full climate modelling is extremely complex, as it has to take account not just of the heating effect of greenhouse gases but of all the ensuing consequences that then feed back into the model. The oceans can absorb heat, as a vast, dark body. As the temperature of the sea rises, ice in and bordering the sea melts, and as the temperature of the air rises, ice on land melts. The melting ice adds water to the oceans, raising the sea level. Rising sea levels mean that more land is underwater, and so the surface area of the ocean is larger. This simultaneously increases the area of dark surface and removes areas of ice that previously helped to reflect heat back from the surface of the Earth. Consequently, melting ice and rising sea levels contribute to an ever-increasing speed of heating. At the same time, removal of forest and other greenery adds to the build-up of CO_2, as its removal through photosynthesis is reduced. Rising temperatures lead to desertification, making land inhospitable to plant life and so further reducing photosynthesis. This, too, fuels an escalating spiral of rising temperatures and raised CO_2 levels. Climate scientists are now almost unanimous in considering human activity to be driving high levels of CO_2 and consequent climate change.

A Timeline: the Before, During and After of the Climate Change Threat

1896 Svante Arrhenuis proposes a link between rising global temperatures and increasing CO_2 in the atmosphere.

1938 Guy Callendar argues that CO_2-triggered global warming is already happening.

1956 Maurice Ewing and William L. Donn suggest a rapid-onset ice age is possible.

1958 It is discovered that a greenhouse effect on Venus has raised the surface temperature to well above the boiling point of water.

1960 Charles Keeling accurately measures the CO_2 in the atmosphere and finds it is rising year on year.

1967 Syukuro Manabe calculates the expected rise from doubling of CO_2 levels as 2°C.

1968 Studies suggest that Antarctic ice sheets could collapse, triggering a catastrophic rise in sea levels.

1973 James Lovelock suggests that CFCs (chlorofluorocarbons) could have a greenhouse effect 10,000 times worse than CO_2.

1977 Scientific opinion fixes on warming as a more likely threat than cooling.

1982 Strong global warming since the mid-1970s is reported, with 1981 the warmest year on record.

1987 Antarctic ice cores show a strong correspondence in the past between high levels of CO_2 and higher temperatures – but current levels are the highest for 400,000 years.

1988 The UN founds the Intergovernmental Panel on Climate Change (IPCC).

1992 The first Earth Summit in Rio de Janeiro calls for world action on climate change.

1997 The Kyoto Protocol seeks to reduce carbon emissions.

2005 The requirements of the Kyoto Protocol come into force, aiming to stabilise greenhouse-gas emissions at levels that will prevent further climate change.

2015 The 21st Conference of the Parties on climate change sets legally binding targets to cut carbon emissions for most countries for post-2020.

NEIL ARMSTRONG BECOMES THE FIRST MAN ON THE MOON

1969

"Here men from the planet Earth first set foot upon the moon July 1969ad. We came in peace for all mankind."

A plaque left on the Apollo 11 lunar module Eagle, the craft that safely transported the first men on to the moon.

In 1961, after the United States had successfully launched Alan Shepard into suborbit for 15 minutes, President John F. Kennedy announced the most ambitious space plan ever proposed: "This nation should commit itself to achieving the goal, before the decade is out, of landing a man on the moon and returning him safely to the Earth." The first step was to match the Soviet achievement of launching a man into orbit. This was finally accomplished on February 20, 1962, when John Glenn became the first U.S. astronaut to orbit the Earth aboard Mercury spacecraft, Friendship 7. Nearly a year after Vostok 1, the U.S. had finally caught up with its Soviet rival. To land a man on the moon, NASA had to be able to dock two spacecraft together in space, which landed with NASA's most experienced pilot, Neil Armstrong.

In March 1966, Armstrong was launched into space aboard Gemini 8, to dock with an unmanned rocket there. However, after catching up to the rocket and successfully docking with it, the two craft went into a spin. Armstrong managed to separate the spacecraft, but Gemini 8 continued to spin out of control. The only solution was to abort the mission and fire Gemini's re-entry thrusters to gain control of the craft. No one was hurt as Gemini 8 made an emergency splashdown into the Pacific Ocean, but the incident was a stark reminder that things could go badly wrong in space.

In January 1967, the United States suffered its first great space tragedy when astronauts Virgil Grissom, Ed White and Roger Chaffee were killed during testing of Apollo 1. Apollo 1 was scheduled to become the first manned Apollo mission into space, and the accident took place during a routine practice run of the spacecraft's launch. The three astronauts had boarded Apollo 1's command module and its hatch was bolted on behind them. Suddenly, a chilling cry came over the radio: "We've got a fire in the cockpit!". The flash fire that swept through the command module reached such an intense heat that all three astronauts were killed within minutes before the hatch could be removed. A report later revealed that NASA had cut corners in its race to get a man to the moon.

In reaction to fears that the Soviet Union was planning a lunar landing, the U.S. launched its first spacecraft to the moon: Apollo 8. On December 21, 1968, Apollo 8 orbited the Earth once before its rockets fired it to an "escape velocity" of 40,234kph (25,000mph) to push it out of Earth's orbit. Less than three days later, Apollo 8's rockets fired again to put it into the moon's orbit. Those at NASA held their breath as Apollo 8 travelled around the moon to its far side – a place never seen by human eyes. Then, to everyone's relief, Apollo 8 emerged on the other side. The astronauts on board then glimpsed something never seen before: the Earth rising above the moon's horizon, or "Earthrise". The United States had proved that the moon was now within its reach.

As Neil Armstrong slowly climbed down the ladder of the Eagle lunar module, he was not exactly sure what lay below. Thousands of scientists, designers and engineers at NASA had sent three men 386,400km (240,000 miles) from Earth to explore a new world for the first time – but nobody could predict what its surface would be like. As millions of TV viewers on Earth held their breath, Armstrong lowered a tentative foot to the ground and then stepped safely on to the lunar soil. Then, there was a collective sigh of relief and joy as Armstrong uttered his immortal words: "That's one small step for [a] man, one giant leap for mankind." The moon landing symbolized America's victory over the Soviet Union in the space race, which had begun over a decade earlier. At that time the race belonged to the Soviets, who seemed to make one space breakthrough after another.

Determined not to be outdone, President John F. Kennedy made the extraordinary claim that America would have a man on the moon by the end of the decade. The experts at NASA did a double-take at this announcement. America had only just launched a man into suborbit and even its top scientists hadn't conceived of a rocket that could fly as far as the moon. However, in 1969, NASA seemed to have fulfilled Kennedy's wish when Apollo 11 blasted its way out of Earth's orbit and towards the moon. But it was not until Armstrong set foot on to the lunar surface that the success of the moon mission was assured. The astronauts left their footprints in the fine, powdery soil for posterity, but some of it found its way back to Earth, as Armstrong explained during his first phone call back on Earth: "Hello, Mom, this is Neil... it was fantastically beautiful. The surface is covered with a black dust, and it got all over our nice, clean, white suits and wouldn't brush off."

———∞◇∞———

A Timeline: the Before, During and After of Landing a Man on the Moon

May 1966 U.S. Surveyor 1 makes the second soft landing on the moon, a few months after Soviet probe Luna 9.

August 1966 Unmanned U.S. Orbiter 1 enters orbit around the moon.

January 1967 Three astronauts are killed in a fire aboard their Apollo 1 command module.

April 1967 Cosmonaut Vladimir Komarov is killed when the parachutes of his Soyuz 1 capsule fail to open on re-entry.

March 1968 The first man in space, cosmonaut Yuri Gagarin, dies in a plane crash.

December 1968 Frank Borman, James Lovell and William Anders begin the first manned journey from the Earth to the moon aboard Apollo 8.

January 1969 Soyuz 4 and 5 perform the first Soviet spacecraft docking.

June 1969 Neil Armstrong and Edwin "Buzz" Aldrin become the first men on the moon while crewmate Michael Collins orbits around it.

April 1970 On its journey to the moon, Apollo 13 suffers from an explosion and its astronauts have to carry out improvised repairs to get home safely.

1971 Moon vehicle the Lunar Rover is used for the first time by Apollo astronauts.

1973 Unmanned Soviet space probe Mars 2 lands on the surface of Mars.

April 1981 The first U.S. Space Shuttle, *Columbia*, is launched into space.

January 1986 Space Shuttle *Challenger* explodes shortly after launch, killing all seven astronauts on board.

1986 Construction begins on the Soviet *Mir* space station.

2000 The first permanent crew move into the International Space Station (ISS).

2001 American millionaire Dennis Tito pays $20 million to become the first space tourist aboard a Russian Soyuz spacecraft.

2004 SpaceShipOne makes the first-ever privately funded, manned space flight.

2014 The European Space Agency's Rosetta probe reaches Comet 67P/Churyumov–Gerasimenko after a ten-year journey.

EXPLORING THE SOLAR SYSTEM – AND FURTHER

1977

"Mars has been flown by, orbited, smacked into, radar examined and rocketed on to, as well as bounced upon, rolled over, shovelled, drilled into, baked and even blasted. Still to come: Mars being stepped on."

Buzz Aldrin, 2013.

In the early 1960s, both the U.S.S.R. and then the U.S.A. sent probes – unmanned spacecraft – to Venus. The earliest craft had a low rate of success, with few even getting to the planet. The first to land, the Soviet Venera 3, returned no data before it was crushed by the Venusian atmosphere. The first to return data from the surface of another planet was Venera 7 in 1970. It reported surface temperatures of 475°C (887°F) and an atmosphere of almost pure carbon dioxide at pressures of 90 times the Earth's atmospheric pressure. Venera 9 visited in 1975 and sent back the first photographs from the surface of another planet. Mars has always been an attractive to planet to explore, being the most Earth-like and often our nearest neighbor (depending on orbits). But until recently, success has been limited.

The U.S.S.R. launched nine missions to Mars between 1960 and 1969, which all failed. In 1971, Mars 2 crashed on Mars and Mars 3 achieved a controlled landing but stopped transmission after 14 seconds. Vikings 1 and 2, launched by NASA in 1975, became the first successful missions to Mars, with landers collecting samples and sending back color photographs of the planet and orbiters mapping the planet. Subsequent Mars trips have left rovers that have returned data over a long period. A priority is to discover whether there has ever been life on Mars.

The Pioneer 10 mission (NASA), launched on March 3, 1972, photographed Jupiter and its moons before heading off towards interstellar space. It ceased communication with Earth in 2003. It is now more than 100 AU (astronomical units) from the sun, but still 68 light years from the next star on its course – it will take two million years to reach it. Pioneer 11, its sister craft, was the first probe to photograph Saturn and investigate the asteroid belt. Both Pioneers carry a plaque on the outside that shows a picture of naked humans, and pictures that aim to show the location of Earth.

Since the mid-1980s, spacecraft have visited a number of comets, asteroids and dwarf planets, either on flyby missions or with landers. Galileo was launched in 1989 to investigate and photograph Jupiter and its moons. It also became the first craft to flyby an asteroid, 951 Gaspra, and to discover an asteroid moon, Dactyl, which orbits 243 Ida. In 2001, the NASA craft NEAR Shoemaker became the first ever to land on an asteroid, 433 Eros. In 2004, Stardust landed on Wild 2 and not only collected samples of rock but, for the first time, returned them to Earth.

From the start of the 1960s, the U.S.A. and the U.S.S.R. were racing to the moon, but they were also both beginning to explore the wider solar system. The most ambitious project was the launch of Voyagers 1 and 2 in 1977. They were set to fly close to all four of the solar system's largest planets – Jupiter, Saturn, Uranus and Neptune – which were about to line up in a way that happens only once in every 176 years. But, beyond that, they would carry on traveling, leaving the solar system and heading out into space and towards other stars.

Now, in the second decade of the 21st century, Voyager 1 has gone further from Earth than any other man-made object. After photographing Jupiter and Saturn, it set a course for interstellar space and is now beyond the heliosheath – the outer limit of the sun's area of influence. Voyager 2 photographed all four large planets and is a little behind Voyager 1. Both Voyagers carry a "Golden Record", a message for any extraterrestrials that might encounter the craft. It contains a library of sounds and greetings from Earth and of images of Earth and human artifacts.

Some people have worried that the Golden Record could be seen as advertising a planet rich in resources that might attract hostile attention; a few even disapprove of the images of naked humans it shows.

The Voyagers' plutonium power supplies have a half-life of 88 years and might run out between 2020 and 2025. Although this will eventually prevent some critical systems from working, and will finally end communication with the Voyagers, the craft will not stop moving. They will continue ever onwards until found or destroyed. On its current trajectory, Voyager 1 will pass within 1.7 light years of another star in 40,000 years. Some of the original Voyager team suggested that just before Voyager runs out of battery power it should be sent an instruction to use its final fuel to change direction and propel it into a solar system, maximizing the slim chances of it being found around 60,000 years in the future.

A Timeline: the Before, During and After of Exploring the Solar System

1961 The Soviet Sputnik 7 makes the first attempt to fly to Venus, but a rocket failure dooms the mission.

1962 NASA's Messenger 2 makes the first successful flyby of Venus at 34,000km (20,740 miles), discovering ground temperatures up to 428°C (802°F).

1965 Venera 3 (U.S.S.R.) is the first object from Earth to impact with another planet; no data is returned as Venus's atmosphere crushes Venera.

1967 Venera 4 returns data on the temperature and pressure of Venus's atmosphere.

1971 Mars 3 (U.S.S.R.) becomes the first spacecraft to land (not crash) on Mars.

1972 Pioneer 10 (USA) is the first spacecraft to enter the asteroid belt.

1978 Pioneer Venus 1 maps the whole surface of Venus, sending photos back to Earth.

1982 Venera 13 returns the first color photographs from Venus.

1989 Magellan (U.S.A.) maps 98 percent of the surface of Venus to a resolution of 100m (328ft).

2001 NEAR Shoemaker (U.S.A.) lands on the asteroid 433 Eros, the first landing on an asteroid.

2003 Communication with Pioneer 10 ceases as power for its radio transmitter runs out.

2004 Stardust (U.S.A.) lands on Wild 2 and collects samples of rock that are returned to Earth.

2005 Hayabusa (Japan) lands on the asteroid 25143 Itokawa and returns samples to Earth.

2008 Phoenix (NASA) finds water ice below the surface of Mars.

2014 Rosetta (European Space Agency) lands on the comet Churyumov–Gerasimenko.

2015 Messenger (NASA) crashes into the surface of Mercury after running out of fuel.

2037 NASA's target date for a manned mission to Mars.

THE CHERNOBYL DISASTER

1986

> "The odds of a meltdown are one in 10,000 years. The plants have safe and reliable controls that are protected from any breakdown with three safety systems."

The Minister of Power and Electrification of Ukraine, Vitali Sklyarov, speaks to *Soviet Life* magazine about Ukraine's nuclear power stations.

Early in the morning of April 26, 1986, hundreds of firefighters were called to contain the fire at the Chernobyl power station following the explosion. The attending firefighters and policemen noticed large pieces of graphite littered on the ground around Chernobyl, some of which were still red hot. However, despite record levels of radioactivity, nobody arriving at Chernobyl was issued with protective clothing. Nearby, people gathered on a railway bridge to watch the burning reactor. As these people commented on the rainbow colors caused by the burning graphite, they were exposed to a 500-roentgen dose of radiation. A dose of 750 roentgens is considered lethal. No one who stood on the "bridge of death" survived.

At 10am on April 27, helicopters began making drops of sand, lead, clay and neutron-absorbing boron on to Chernobyl's burning reactor, as the people of Pripyat were put on evacuation standby. However, of the 5,000 tons of material dropped on the reactor, almost none of the boron reached the core. By midday, the radiation levels had dropped enough at Chernobyl for authorities to re-evaluate an evacuation. But by 2pm radiation levels were up once more, and the 43,000 residents of Pripyat were evacuated aboard 1,200 buses.

On May 2, it was feared that molten graphite would reach the large pools beneath the still-burning reactor. It was thought that these pools, which were used as water reserves for the reactor's cooling pumps, could then create a steam explosion and eject more radioactive debris into the atmosphere. The three men who volunteered to drain the pools had to work underwater in total darkness, and died shortly afterwards from radiation poisoning. To reduce the risk of the molten reactor core mixing with water from the water table and creating a steam explosion, liquid nitrogen was pumped into the soil beneath the reactor. Thousands of Russian soldiers, known as "bio-robots", were then brought in to collect the worst of the radioactive debris from the reactor. Many were exposed to over 100 times the radiation limits considered safe for humans, and died as a result.

To prevent any further release of radioactive material, a concrete sarcophagus was built over the Chernobyl reactor in December 1986. Constructed from 300,000 tons of concrete and 6,000 tons of steel, the sarcophagus would supposedly protect the environment from radiation for at least 30 years. Construction of the sarcophagus was the biggest engineering project in history and involved 250,000 workers, all of whom reached their official lifetime limits of radiation during the job and received a medal for their efforts. The sarcophagus was later found to be structurally unsafe and leaking radiation. A new archway roof was commissioned in 2007 to replace it.

Events leading up to the explosion at Chernobyl, the worst disaster in the history of nuclear power, began during routine testing of the power station. In the early hours of April 26, 1986, night technicians at Chernobyl's number four reactor shut down its power regulating system and removed the control rods from its core. The reactor then experienced a power surge that caused it to overheat and set off several explosions. These led to a large explosion at 1:23am that blew the steel and concrete lid off the reactor, set the station on fire and caused a partial meltdown. A plume of smoke containing large amounts of radioactive debris then rose high into the atmosphere and blew north. Within a few days the nuclear fallout had passed over much of Europe. The Soviet Union attempted a cover-up, but Scandinavian monitoring stations that had recorded the fallout demanded to know what had happened.

On April 28, the Soviet government admitted there had been an explosion at Chernobyl and a public outcry in Europe ensued. Many people from the nearby city of Pripyat had watched the rising smoke from the power station, as firefighters desperately tried to put out the blaze. The next day, the residents of Pripyat went about their daily lives unaware of the danger. It took 36 hours after the explosion for an evacuation to be ordered. People from Pripyat and its outlying villages were then told to pack supplies for three days and to leave their pets behind. Many assumed they would be back within a few days but most of them would never return to their homes, which today make up the ghost town of Pripyat. Within three months, 31 people had died from the initial effects of Chernobyl, but the true legacy of its radioactive fallout is unknown. Conservative estimates put the death toll from Chernobyl-associated cancers and other diseases in the tens of thousands.

—⁓∘◇∘⁓—

A Timeline: the Before, During and After of the Chernobyl Disaster

1970 Construction of the Chernobyl nuclear power plant and the nearby "atom town" of Pripyat begins.

1976 Filling of the cooling water pools for the Chernobyl power plant begins.

1982 A partial core meltdown occurs in Chernobyl's number one reactor, but the accident is covered up until 1986.

1983 The construction of Chernobyl's number four reactor is completed.

April 25, 1986 A test begins on Chernobyl's number four reactor to observe the reactor under limited power flow.

1:23am, April 26, 1986 The reactor reaches 120 times its full power and explodes, firing radioactive debris into the atmosphere.

1:35am, April 26, 1986 Firefighters arrive to fight the fires on the roof of the turbine hall.

6:35am, April 26, 1986 A total of 186 firefighters from 37 fire brigades extinguish all the fires except the one in the number four reactor.

8pm, April 26, 1986 A government committee arrives to see pieces of graphite on the ground.

12:10am, April 27, 1986 Buses arrive in Pripyat and spend the night waiting for the command to evacuate the city.

7am, April 27, 1986 General Pikalov establishes that the graphite in the reactor is burning, releasing lethal levels of radiation.

2pm, April 27, 1986 The evacuation of Pripyat begins.

April 28, 1986 Moscow television news announces that an accident has occurred at Chernobyl.

July 1986 Chernobyl director Viktor Petrovich Bryukanov is sentenced to ten years in prison for "serious errors and shortcomings in the work that lead to the accident with severe consequences".

November 1986 Chernobyl's number two reactor is restarted.

1987 It is revealed that the Chernobyl disaster has cost the Soviet government over two billion dollars.

1991 A fire breaks out in Chernobyl's number two reactor, causing the roof to collapse.

2007 A new concrete archway sarcophagus is commissioned to replace the existing containment structure over Chernobyl's number four reactor.

POLITICS
AND WAR

Germany Invades Poland

Winston Churchill becomes British Minister

Hiroshima

The Cuban Missile Crisis

John F. Kennedy gets Shot

The Fall of the Berlin Wall

The Collapse of the Soviet Union

GERMANY INVADES POLAND

1939

"...for the second time in our history a British prime minister has returned from Germany bringing peace with honor. I believe it is peace for our time."

British prime minister Neville Chamberlain tells Britain that giving Hitler the Sudetenland has prevented a new war in Europe.

The First World War's Treaty of Versailles had taken away Germany's Rhineland, a strip of land that lay between France, Germany and the Low Countries (the region of northwest Europe that includes the Netherlands, Belgium and Luxembourg), which contained many industrial centres that Adolf Hitler needed to build up his military. In March 1936, in direct violation of the Treaty of Versailles, which stated that the Rhineland should remain a demilitarized zone, Hitler ordered his troops to occupy the Rhineland. Despite this breach of the treaty, neither Britain nor France mounted a response, which underlined their ineffective system of appeasement towards the Nazis.

After Hitler's success in occupying the Rhineland, he next targeted the Sudetenland, an area in Czechoslovakia with a large German population. The Sudetenland Germans were coaxed into staging a revolt on secret orders passed down from Hitler, who then insisted that the Sudetenland become part of Germany. Although the uprising was put down by the Czechoslovakian army, British prime minister Neville Chamberlain flew to Germany to discuss the Sudetenland with Hitler in September 1938. After talks between Britain, France, Germany and Italy, it was agreed that Germany could have the Sudetenland on condition that it left the rest of Czechoslovakia alone. Chamberlain saw this agreement as a victory in ensuring peace in Europe. Hitler, on the other hand, ignored the terms and ordered his troops to enter Prague in March 1939. Czechoslovakia had become part of Germany.

In April 1939, Britain and France attempted to form a pact with Russia to come to Poland's defense if it was invaded by Germany. The terms of the agreement were not easily met: British prime minister Neville Chamberlain disliked Soviet leader Joseph Stalin, and Stalin did not trust France and Britain to stand up to Germany. Poland said it would not allow Soviet troops access through Poland to attack Germany, and the talks stalled. In the meantime, Stalin formed a secret pact with Hitler in August 1939, to attack Poland and divide it up between them.

After the invasion of Poland, Polish Jews were confined to ghettos and sent to concentration camps. The first concentration camps were built in 1933, and they became the sites of mass murder where millions were starved, tortured, worked to death or executed. Many of the largest concentration camps were built in Nazi-occupied Poland, including Auschwitz II-Birkenau, which was designed for the mass extermination of Jews, homosexuals, Roma people and anyone else the Third Reich considered inferior. Over six million Jews were murdered in Nazi death camps, which were created to carry out Hitler's "Final Solution" – the systematic murder of all Jews in Europe.

Hitler's invasion of Poland began without warning, provocation or declaration of war, and it unleashed the full force of the German army on to the militarily inferior Poles. At 4:45am on September 1, 1939, 1.5 million German soldiers supported by tanks and cavalry attacked Poland on several fronts. From 6am, bombing raids commenced, as over 1,300 aircraft began their Blitzkrieg on Polish cities, roads and railway junctions. Towns and villages were deliberately targeted so that panicked civilians would flee their homes and block the main transport arteries. German air supremacy was achieved in a matter of hours as most of the Polish airforce was caught unawares on the ground. After the Luftwaffe (the German airforce) had dropped its bombs, Panzer divisions destroyed the lines of Polish defense ahead of the 62 German infantry divisions that followed behind. The Polish army, which included cavalry divisions armed with sabers, was no match for the German war machine.

By September 8, a few Polish army strongholds remained around Pomerania, Poznan, Lodz, Krakow and Carpathia, but these were quickly bombed into submission. After only eight days of invasion, the German tanks were at the outskirts of Warsaw. A last stand in eastern Poland was called, but its success would have only been made possible with help from British and French forces, which did not arrive. The allies' promise to come to Poland's aid in the face of Nazi aggression was as worthless as its policy of appeasement towards Hitler – a policy the dictator had counted on when attacking Poland. Britain and France finally declared war on Germany on September 3, at 5pm, two days after the invasion of Poland had begun. On September 17, all hope of Polish resistance fell when the Soviet Red Army crossed the Polish border, in fulfilment of a secret pact with Hitler. After bravely holding out for 18 days of continuous bombing, Warsaw finally surrendered on September 27. Poland had fallen.

A Timeline: the During and After of Germany Invading Poland

September 1, 1939 Germany invades Poland.

September 3, 1939 Britain and France declare war on Germany.

September 17, 1939 The Soviet Union invades Poland.

September 27, 1939 Poland surrenders to Germany.

May 1940 Churchill becomes prime minister of Britain as Germany advances to western Europe.

June 1940 German troops enter Paris.

July 1940 The Luftwaffe begin the Battle of Britain.

June 1941 Hitler invades the Soviet Union.

December 1941 Japan attacks Pearl Harbor. Germany and Italy declare war on the U.S.

January 1942 Details of the Final Solution are mapped out at the Wannsee Conference.

February 1943 The German army in Stalingrad surrenders.

May 1943 The German and Italian armies in north Africa surrender.

September 1943 Allied troops invade Italy.

January 1944 The Germans are defeated at Leningrad after a 900-day siege.

June 1944 D-Day: the Allied invasion of Nazi-occupied Europe begins.

June 1994 The first German V-2 rockets are launched at Britain.

August 1944 The Warsaw uprising begins.

January 1945 The Auschwitz II-Birkenau death camp is liberated, revealing the true horrors of Hitler's war to the world.

May 1945 Germany signs its unconditional surrender.

August 1945 The U.S. drops atomic bombs on the Japanese cities of Hiroshima and Nagasaki. The Japanese sign their unconditional surrender in September, signalling the end of the war.

WINSTON CHURCHILL BECOMES BRITISH PRIME MINISTER

1940

"Let us therefore brace ourselves to our duties, and so bear ourselves that, if the British Empire and its Commonwealth last for a thousand years, men will still say, 'This was their finest hour.'"

Winston Churchill delivers his "Finest Hour" speech to the House of Commons on June 18, 1945.

Winston Churchill's high-risk decision to rescue Allied troops, forced to the beaches of Dunkirk by the German advance, formed part of his determination for Britain to fight on alone. Around 338,000 men were evacuated, in what Churchill called "a miracle of deliverance". Reporting on this in the House of Commons, he declared, "We shall fight on the beaches...we shall fight in the fields and in the streets...We shall never surrender."

In the summer of 1940, the Battle of Britain raged in the skies above the south coast of England and inland to London. A turning point came with a fight over the capital, in which the Luftwaffe lost 61 planes to the RAF's 31. While Churchill was visiting Fighter Command at RAF Uxbridge, Londoners watched the battle raging overhead. Germany soon abandoned daylight raids and two days later Hitler postponed his planned invasion of Britain. The selfless contribution of RAF pilots, whose average age was about 20, was summed up for all time by Churchill: "Never, in the field of human conflict, was so much owed by so many to so few."

Against the backdrop of Fascist tyranny, Churchill met President Roosevelt in Placentia Bay, Newfoundland, to construct a set of principles for a peaceful postwar world. This document, signed by both, was called the Atlantic Charter and was formally adopted at the founding of the United Nations Organization in San Francisco, in 1945. Its principles included the right of nations to safety and sovereignty, and of all citizens to live in "freedom from fear and want".

Two months after the Anglo-American landings in North Africa, Churchill met Roosevelt to co-ordinate plans for victory over the Axis powers (Germany, Italy and Japan). It was the first of several such conferences. Churchill prevailed with his aim of completing the German defeat in North Africa, to be followed by an invasion of Sicily. Both agreed to postpone D-Day to the following year, but meanwhile to deliver aid to the Soviet Union and conduct a major bombing campaign of German cities.

By May 1940, Britain and her allies were losing the war against Hitler. As the Nazis marched across Europe and one nation after another fell before the German jackboots, Britain needed a wartime prime minister to replace the weak and indecisive Neville Chamberlain. That man was Winston Churchill, the iconic leader who shone like a beacon of hope as Britain and Europe faced its darkest days. Five weeks after Churchill became prime minister, minister of defence and the leader responsible for Britain's war effort, he delivered his "Finest Hour" speech to the nation. Churchill was famed for his rousing oratory, and his speech insisted that the people of Britain stand up and fight the Germans, as "Hitler knows that he will have to break us in this island or lose the war". Churchill later wrote that, at 65 years old, his moment for "walking with destiny" had come, a moment that his previous careers as a soldier, journalist and politician had prepared him for.

Churchill's courage, spirit and energy gave inestimable inspiration to his isolated people, as France fell and his country faced the Battle of Britain and the German Blitzkrieg (German air raids). Hitler's defeat in the Battle of Britain ruined his plans for the invasion of Britain – "Operation Sea Lion" – and represented a turning point in the war. Enraged, Hitler continued to try and destroy London through his Luftwaffe's Blitzkrieg, which destroyed over one million houses in 1940 alone. The Blitz was another defining moment for Churchill, who visited the areas reduced to rubble, often dressed in a boiler suit, to shake the hands of survivors and promise them victory was on its way.

As one of the "Big Three" Allied commanders, Churchill shaped military strategy with Joseph Stalin and Roosevelt against the Nazis and helped to redefine Europe's borders at the end of the war. Churchill was the first British statesman of the 20th century to be honored with a state funeral.

———◦◦◇◦◦——

A Timeline: the Life, Experience and Influence of Winston Churchill

November 30, 1874 Winston Leonard Spencer Churchill is born at Blenheim Palace, Oxfordshire, UK, to his American mother Jennie Jerome (born in Brooklyn).

November 1899 Working as a journalist during the Boer War, Churchill is captured but escapes on December 12, becoming a national hero.

October 24, 1900 Churchill is elected Conservative MP for Oldham and begins his parliamentary career.

February 19, 1910 Having switched allegiance to the Liberal Party in 1904, Churchill becomes Home Secretary in the Asquith government.

September 3, 1939 Britain declares war on Germany. Churchill is appointed First Lord of the Admiralty in the War Cabinet.

September 27, 1939 Poland surrenders to Germany.

May 10, 1940 Churchill becomes Prime Minister of an all-party coalition government, and self-appointed Minister for Defence.

June 22, 1940 France surrenders to Germany, which has now overrun most of Europe.

August 24, 1940 London is bombed by the German Luftwaffe for the first time. Outraged, Churchill orders the RAF to bomb Berlin 24 hours later.

September 7, 1940 The Blitz on London begins on "Black Saturday" with a 12-hour attack in which 430 people are killed. The following day, Churchill visits the East End to inspect the damage and doubles the capital's air defenses.

October 23–November 5, 1942 Newly appointed by Churchill, Lieutenant-General Bernard Montgomery, commanding the Eighth Army in North Africa, defeats General Erwin Rommel at the Second Battle of El Alamein.

May 8, 1945 Churchill announces the unconditional surrender of Germany.

July 5, 1945 General Election defeat by Labour, but Churchill remains leader of the Opposition.

October 25, 1951 Churchill is re-elected Prime Minister at the head of a Conservative government. He resigns in 1955 due to ill health.

January 24, 1965 Churchill dies in London, age 90.

HIROSHIMA

1945

"The atom bomb was no 'great decision'. It was merely another powerful weapon in the arsenal of righteousness."

U.S. president Harry S. Truman speaks about the atomic bombs he ordered to be dropped on Japan during the Second World War.

In 1939, Albert Einstein wrote to U.S. president Franklin D. Roosevelt to tell him that developments in nuclear physics had opened the way for the design of an atomic weapon. Roosevelt immediately ordered a top-secret military program to create the bomb, which would give the Allied powers an unstoppable advantage over Germany. The resulting program became the "Manhattan" in 1942 and it included top physicists from Allied countries around the world. After the program was able to successfully create a bomb, new U.S. president Harry S. Truman wrote in his diary, "We have discovered the most terrible bomb in the history of the world." The two bombs the scientists built – Little Boy and Fat Man – caused massive loss of life, the end of the Second World War and the beginning of a new, nuclear age.

As increasing Allied victories over Germany drew the war in Europe to a close, Japan showed no signs of ending its hostilities. To bomb the country into submission, the U.S. dropped over 2,000 tons of incendiary bombs on Tokyo on March 9, 1945. The bombs created vast firestorms that destroyed almost 41 sq km (16 sq miles) of the Japanese capital and killed between 80,000 and 130,000 civilians. The stench of burning human flesh was reportedly so strong that the American bomber pilots were forced to wear oxygen masks to stop them from vomiting as they delivered their payloads over the city.

After the war in Europe had ended, U.S. president Harry S. Truman met British prime minister Winston Churchill and Soviet leader Joseph Stalin at the Potsdam Conference in July 1945. The conference was designed to redraw Europe's borders and also discuss what to do about Japan. At the end of July, the Allies issued a declaration to Japan asking it to surrender or otherwise face "utter destruction". Unaware of America's new atomic capabilities, Japan decided not to comply with the threat.

On September 2, 1945, Japan signed the official document detailing its unconditional surrender. It followed the devastating "Fat Boy" bomb being dropped on the city of Nagasaki on August 9. Although the bomb was more powerful than the "Little Boy" dropped on Hiroshima, the impact of the blast was partially contained by the hills surrounding the city. Despite this, between 40,000 and 80,000 people were killed by the explosion. Even after the devastation of Hiroshima and Nagasaki, the Japanese government was still divided on whether to surrender. However, Emperor Hirohito intervened to prevent any more loss of Japanese life. When Hirohito made a radio announcement on August 15 that Japan would surrender, it was the first time many people had heard his voice. Hiroshima was later rebuilt as a peace memorial.

At 8:15am on August 6, 1945, the United States dropped "the most terrible bomb in the history of the world" on the Japanese city of Hiroshima. The first atomic bomb ever used in warfare was delivered by B-29 bomber the *Enola Gay* and exploded in a blinding flash of light 580m (1,902ft) above the ground. From its point of impact, the bomb destroyed over 16 sq km (6 sq miles) of the city and produced a wave of heat so intense that many people were simply vaporized where they stood. Between 60,000 and 80,000 people were killed instantly in the bomb blast.

The initial blast was followed by violent winds that caused a series of firestorms to rage for three days throughout the remains of the city. Thousands of people who had survived the explosion were killed in the fires that followed it. Those who were left alive tried to flee the city, but many later succumbed to their injuries and the radiation sickness caused by exposure to the bomb. In the end, Hiroshima's death toll stood at 135,000. Hiroshima had been chosen as a target by U.S. president Harry S. Truman because it had not previously been bombed during America's raids on Japan. It therefore provided an unscarred model that would show the full damage that an atomic weapon could inflict on a city.

America had used the atomic bomb because it feared that a ground invasion of Japan would cause an even greater loss of life. It hoped Japan would quickly agree to an unconditional surrender after experiencing America's destructive new weapon and thus bring an end to the Second World War. However, three days after Hiroshima, the Japanese government had made no move to surrender. In response, the U.S. dropped another atomic bomb on the city of Nagasaki. The Japanese surrendered shortly afterwards, on September 2, 1945. The Second World War was officially over.

—◦∞◦—

A Timeline: the Before, During and After of Hiroshima

1940 President Franklin D. Roosevelt orders research to begin into building an atomic weapon.

September 1940 Japan, Germany and Italy sign the Tripartite Pact, strengthening their ties against the Allies.

December 1941 Japan's invasion of Thailand and its attacks on British-controlled Malaya, Singapore and Hong Kong starts the war in the Pacific.

December 1941 Japan attacks the Pearl Harbor U.S. naval base in Hawaii, bringing America into the war.

February 1945 With the Nazi defeat in sight, Joseph Stalin, Franklin D. Roosevelt and Winston Churchill meet at the Yalta conference to discuss Germany's fate.

March 1945 America orders an intensive bombing raid on Tokyo, resulting in devastating firestorms.

April 1945 Harry S. Truman becomes president of the United States after the death of Franklin D. Roosevelt.

May 1945 Germany signs the document offering its unconditional surrender to the Allies.

May 8, 1945 VE or "Victory in Europe" Day is celebrated in the cities of Europe.

June 1945 The Americans win the 82-day-long battle of Okinawa against the Japanese.

July 1945 The first atomic bomb is successfully exploded in an American test in Albuquerque, New Mexico.

July 1945 Japanese Emperor Hirohito asks his government to consider surrender, but it declines to do so.

August 6, 1945 The United States drops an atomic bomb on Hiroshima.

August 9, 1945 The United States drops an atomic bomb on Nagasaki.

August 9, 1945 The Soviet Union enters the war against Japan by invading Japanese-held Manchuria.

August 15, 1945 The effects of the Soviet entry into the war against Japan and the atomic bombings of Hiroshima and Nagasaki lead to Japan announcing its surrender. It is known today as VJ or "Victory in Japan" Day.

September 2, 1945 Japan signs its official document of unconditional surrender.

1946 The international military tribunal for the Far East begins its investigations into Japanese war crimes.

THE CUBAN MISSILE CRISIS

1962

MEDIUM RANGE BALLISTIC MISSILE BASE IN CUBA
SAN CRISTOBAL

"If you weigh the present situation with a cool head without giving way to passion, you will understand that the Soviet Union cannot afford not to decline the despotic demands of the USA."

Telegram from Soviet premier Nikita Khrushchev to U.S. President John F. Kennedy, explaining why American "piracy" in Cuban waters would lead to war.

On October 22, 1962, President John F. Kennedy made a televised announcement to the American public explaining that he had ordered a blockade around Cuba and would use military force against Soviet ships entering Cuban waters. On the same day, U.S. diplomats met with the leaders of Canada, Britain, West Germany and France to brief them on the blockade. All responded that they were supportive of the U.S. position. In Moscow, U.S. ambassador Foy D. Kohler briefed Khrushchev on the pending blockade. The people of the world took a deep, collective breath and waited for news. Many Americans began hoarding water, food and petrol in preparation for a nuclear war.

On the evening of October 24, details of a telegram from Khrushchev to Kennedy were broadcast by Soviet news agency TASS. In the telegram, Khrushchev stated that the Soviet Union viewed the blockade as "an act of aggression" and their ships would be instructed to ignore it. On the same day, Pope John XXIII sent an imploring message to the Kremlin that said, "We beg all governments not to remain deaf to this cry of humanity. That they do all that is in their power to save peace." The next day, the Pope's message was broadcast worldwide on the radio. While having no direct impact on the negotiations, the pope's message did allow both leaders to stand back from the conflict without losing face. The message also marked the first climax of the conflict, one that enabled further discussions to be held between Washington and Moscow.

As the United States military went to DEFCON 2, it sent 23 nuclear-armed B-52 bombers to points within striking distance of the Soviet Union and put 145 intercontinental ballistic missiles on ready alert. Then the world waited as the first ships approached the U.S. blockade. After letting oil tanker the *Bucharest* through the blockade, U.S. warships boarded the Lebanese *Marucla* to inspect its cargo and let it pass. American intelligence reported that there had been no slow-down on the building of Soviet bases on Cuba, although the Soviet Union had turned back 14 of its ships en route to Cuba.

The crisis looked certain to come to a head after a U.S. spy plane was shot down over Cuba on October 27. Believing that the surface-to-air missile must have been launched by the Soviets, the U.S. readied a Cuban invasion force in Florida. But then, on the brink of attack, Kennedy changed his mind and decided to give the Soviets the benefit of the doubt. It was later learned that Khrushchev had ordered no Soviet missiles be fired against U.S. aircraft, as he assumed this would escalate the conflict into war. From that moment on, a way out of the crisis would be found through diplomacy.

⚜

In October 1962, the United States stood on the brink of war with the Soviet Union after discovering the presence of Soviet nuclear missiles in Cuba. The trouble began in May 1960, when Soviet premier Nikita Khrushchev began delivering missiles to Cuba after promising to defend the island against hostile attack. In August, a U.S. U-2 spy plane reported new Soviet military constructions on the island. Then, in October, spy-plane photos showed a ballistic missile standing on a launch pad. A ballistic missile launched from Cuba had the capability of hitting America within minutes, and its presence was taken as an overtly hostile act that the U.S. could not ignore. After considering an invasion of Cuba, or airstrikes against the new missile bases, President John F. Kennedy instead ordered a military blockade or "quarantine" around Cuba on October 22. Kennedy then informed Khrushchev that the U.S. would seize any offensive military material en route from Russia to Cuba.

Over the next few days, Soviet ships bound for Cuba diverted away from the quarantine zone as tension mounted on both the Soviet and U.S. sides. As the world teetered on the brink of nuclear war, Khrushchev and Kennedy exchanged letters and telegrams. On October 28, seven days after the crisis began, Khrushchev capitulated. He told Kennedy that the Soviet bases on Cuba would be dismantled and the missiles returned to the Soviet Union. In response, Kennedy said that the U.S. would never invade Cuba and promised to withdraw the nuclear missiles it had been stockpiling in Turkey. As the two nations began to fulfil their promises, Cuban leader Fidel Castro raged against Khrushchev's apparent unwillingness to stand up to the Americans. Many Soviet officials felt the same way, and in October 1964, Khrushchev fell from power. However, he had succeeded in steering his country through one of the greatest crises of the 20th century: at no other time had the United States and the Soviet Union looked so close to war.

—◦◦◇◦◦—

A Timeline: the Before, During and After of the Cuban Missile Crisis

January 1959 Fidel Castro assumes power after the Cuban Revolution and aligns Cuba with the Soviet Union.

October 1959 Turkey and the United States agree to deploy 15 Jupiter missiles in Turkey in 1961.

May 1960 The Soviet Union and Cuba establish diplomatic relations. The United States ends its foreign-aid program to Cuba.

August 1960 The United States begins a trade embargo against Cuba.

January 1961 John F. Kennedy is inaugurated as the 35th president of the United States.

April 1961 A group of Cuban exiles backed by the U.S. invades Cuba at the Bay of Pigs, but fails to trigger an anti-Castro revolution.

January 1962 U.S. intelligence reveals Soviet missile deliveries to Cuba.

September 1962 Soviet foreign minister Andrei Gromyko warns America that an attack on Cuba could mean war with the Soviet Union.

October 14, 1962 A U.S. U-2 spy plane takes photos of Soviet missile sites on Cuba.

October 22, 1962 Soviet foreign minister Andrei Gromyko tells Kennedy that any Soviet weapons in Cuba are only to strengthen the "defensive capabilities of Cuba".

October 22, 1962 U.S. military forces go to DEFCON 3 (defence readiness condition three out of a possible five) as congressional leaders are shown the photos of the Soviet missile installations in Cuba.

October 22, 1962 Kennedy forms the Executive Committee of the National Security Council (ExComm) to advise him during the crisis.

October 24, 1962 Pope John XXIII implores the Kremlin not to start a nuclear war.

October 25, 1962 Now on DEFCOM 2, for the only time in U.S. history, the military puts its nuclear-armed B-52 bombers on continuous airborne alert.

October 26, 1962 Khrushchev sends a letter to President Kennedy proposing to remove his missiles if Kennedy says he will never invade Cuba.

October 27, 1962 An American U-2 is shot down over Cuba.

October 27, 1962 Kennedy sends Khrushchev a letter saying the U.S. will not invade Cuba if Khrushchev removes his missiles.

October 28, 1962 Khrushchev announces that he has agreed to remove the Soviet missiles from Cuba.

JOHN F. KENNEDY GETS SHOT

1963

"My fellow Americans, ask not what your country can do for you, ask what you can do for your country."

John F. Kennedy makes his inauguration address in 1961, the shortest in U.S. history at 13 minutes and 42 seconds long.

After failing his military medical, John Kennedy asked his father Joseph to pull some political strings to enable him to join the navy in 1941. After attending an officers' training course, Kennedy was given command of a patrol boat in 1942 and stationed in the south Pacific. In 1943, while on night patrol near the Solomon Islands, Kennedy's PT-109 boat collided with a Japanese destroyer. Two of Kennedy's men were killed instantly, but he managed to lead the remaining members through the sea to a nearby island. He then returned to the wreck to save a last, badly burned man. These brave actions won Kennedy the Navy and Marine Corps Medal and made him a war hero back in the United States.

While on the presidential campaign trail in 1960, Kennedy faced questions on a range of tough issues. By the time Kennedy participated with Republican candidate Richard Nixon in the first-ever televised presidential debate, the two candidates were neck and neck. However, television was where Kennedy came into his own. During the debate, the young and charismatic Kennedy appeared calm and confident compared to Nixon, who was visibly uncomfortable under the glare of the lights and cameras. The debate helped tip the election Kennedy's way and gave birth to a new media-savvy brand of politics that was later emulated by future presidents Bill Clinton and Barack Obama.

Only three months after his inauguration, Kennedy suffered embarrassment at home and abroad after 1,500 CIA-trained Cuban exiles failed in their attempt to invade Cuba on April 17, 1961. Approved by Kennedy, the Cuban invasion was quickly thwarted by the country's army and failed in its aims to mount an island-wide insurrection against its communist leader, Fidel Castro. Kennedy was able to re-establish his foreign-policy credibility during the Cuban Missile Crisis at the end of 1962. The young president showed his willingness to use military power against his adversary Nikita Khrushchev by blocking the delivery of Soviet missiles to Cuba, and then used diplomatic avenues to avert a nuclear war.

Kennedy was at the height of his popularity when he was assassinated in 1963. The route Kennedy's motorcade took on its journey through Dallas had been publicized so well-wishers could gather to welcome her. As the procession passed the Texas School Book Depository, a lone gunman, Lee Harvey Oswald, fired three lethal shots into the car. Oswald was found hiding in a theater 80 minutes later and was duly arrested, but was himself shot and killed by Jack Ruby the next day while in police custody. Ruby then died of pneumonia in 1966, while awaiting trial. The motives of both men, and the many conspiracy theories that surround Kennedy's death, continue to the present day.

At 12:30 on November 22, 1963, shots rang out in downtown Dallas. The bullets struck American president John F. Kennedy in the neck and head as he travelled to a speaking engagement in an open-top limousine. He was pronounced dead shortly after arriving at a nearby hospital. Kennedy's assassination stunned the United States. A dynamic and popular president, Kennedy had presided over Cold War tensions with the Soviet Union and introduced groundbreaking domestic reforms, such as the expansion of civil rights to black Americans. Kennedy's ascent to power, however, had not been easy.

Born into a wealthy Irish-American family, Kennedy entered politics after returning from the Second World War a naval war hero. Bankrolled by his ex-ambassador father Joseph, Kennedy was elected to the U.S. House of Representatives in 1946 and then the Senate in 1952. Although he kept a charming and energetic demeanor in public, behind the scenes Kennedy was plagued with health issues, including back problems and Addison's disease, which left him in constant pain. Despite taking steroids and amphetamines for pain relief, Kennedy won the Democrat party's presidential nomination in 1960 and defeated Richard Nixon in the election that same year.

Kennedy's campaign had introduced America to an entirely new form of presidential politics, one based around the cult of personality rather than a figurehead toeing the party line. Kennedy was also America's youngest president at 43 years old and its first Roman Catholic. Many expected Kennedy to falter during the Cuban Missile Crisis, which occurred only two years into his presidency, but Kennedy saw off the crisis and his critics by averting war through diplomacy. He then announced that the U.S. would defeat the Soviets in the space race by being the first nation to put a man on the moon. This would take place by Kennedy's own deadline of 1969, six years after his assassination.

A Timeline: the Life, Experience and Influence of the John F. Kennedy

1936 John F. Kennedy attends Harvard University.

1938–9 Kennedy tours Europe.

1940 Kennedy's thesis is published as *Why England Slept*.

1945 Kennedy is discharged from the U.S. Navy.

1946 Kennedy is elected to the House of Representatives.

1952 Kennedy defeats Henry Cabot Lodge to win election to the United States Senate.

1953 Kennedy marries glamorous socialite, Jacqueline Bouvier.

July 1960 Kennedy wins the Democratic nomination for president and picks Lyndon B. Johnson as his running mate.

1961 Kennedy defeats Richard Nixon and becomes the 35th president of the United States.

March 1961 Kennedy announces the establishment of the Peace Corps.

April 1961 An American-backed invasion of Cuba ends in disaster at the Bay of Pigs.

June 1961 Kennedy and Nikita Khrushchev hold a summit in Vienna.

October 22, 1962 Kennedy announces a naval quarantine of Cuba after a spy plane finds evidence of Soviet missiles on the island.

October 22, 1962 The Soviet Union agrees to remove its missiles from Cuba.

June 1963 Kennedy calls the black civil-rights struggle a "moral crisis" for America.

August 1963 The United States and the Soviet Union agree to a nuclear test-ban treaty.

November 1963 An American-backed coup overthrows the government of south Vietnam and replaces it with a military dictatorship.

November 22, 1963 Kennedy is assassinated in Dallas, Texas, and Johnson is sworn in as president.

THE FALL OF THE BERLIN WALL

1989

"Nobody has the intention of building a wall."

GDR head of state Walter Ulbricht speaks at a press
conference in East Berlin on June 15,1961, just weeks
before barriers are erected between East and West Berlin.

In 1949, Germany was divided into the Federal Republic of Germany
(FRG), in the west, and the German Democratic Republic (GDR), in the
east. This caused an exodus of around 2.5 million East Germans to the
west between 1949 and 1961. Fearing it was losing its best and brightest
workers to the democratic west, the GDR built a barrier in Berlin to close
off access for East Germans. First erected on the night of August 12,
the original wall was constructed from barbed wire and cinder blocks,
but these were later replaced by a series of 5-m (16-ft) high concrete
walls topped with barbed wire, watchtowers and gun emplacements.
By 1980, the Berlin Wall stretched for 45km (28 miles) through Berlin
and extended for another 121km (75 miles) around West Berlin, cutting
it off from East Germany. In 1987, U.S. president Ronald Reagan asked
Soviet Union leader Mikhail Gorbachev to tear down the Berlin Wall as
a symbol of increasing freedom across Soviet Europe.

In 1989, the Hungarian government dismantled the barbed-wire fences along its borders with Austria and thousands of East Germans illegally crossed into the country. Mass demonstrations then began in East Germany, the most notable of which was a large protest held by 500,000 people in East Berlin's Alexanderplatz. In reaction, East Germany's leader Erich Honecker resigned on October 18, 1989, and was replaced by Egon Krenz. Realizing that he could not stop the flow of East Germans escaping into Austria and Czechoslovakia, Krenz decided to allow border crossing between East and West Germany, including in Berlin. He left it to unofficial spokesperson Günter Schabowski to announce the news.

As the power of the Soviet Union in Europe began to crumble, an historic meeting took place between the leaders of the Cold War nations, the United States and the Soviet Union. On December 3, 1989, U.S. President George H. W. Bush met Soviet leader Mikhail Gorbachev aboard Soviet ship the SS *Maxim Gorkiy* off the coast of Malta. During this "Malta Summit", the two leaders agreed to officially end the Cold War that had begun four decades earlier and at times threatened to plunge the world into nuclear devastation. Pieces of the Berlin Wall were handed out by Bush at the end of the summit.

In July 1990, East Germany formally adopted the currency of West Germany and all border controls between the two halves of the country ended. This marked the start of German reunification, which reached its conclusion 95 days later on October 3, 1990. Not everyone was happy about the reunification: British prime minister Margaret Thatcher had asked Gorbachev to stop it happening, saying it would undermine the security of Europe. French president François Mitterrand had also voiced his concern, telling Thatcher that a reunified Germany could potentially be more dangerous than Nazi Germany. The people of Germany disagreed and came out in force on November 9, 1990, to celebrate the one-year anniversary of the fall of the Berlin Wall, and the birth of a new democratic Europe.

On the evening of April 9, 1989, an astonishing announcement was made on German television. During a press conference that day, East German spokesperson Günter Schabowski had declared that the checkpoint crossings in the Berlin Wall would be opened for the first time in 28 years. But when he was pressed on when this would take effect, Schabowski appeared flummoxed. He reread the note given to him by his party superiors and then replied, "As far as I know, effective immediately, without delay." It was a classic bureaucratic blunder: no one had told Schabowski that the regulation was to come into force the next day, and suddenly, without warning, Schabowski had inadvertently all but announced the end of the Cold War.

Tens of thousands of East Berliners subsequently flocked to the Berlin Wall checkpoint crossings, where confused guards, who knew nothing about the news, wondered how they would hold back the increasingly large crowd. In the end, just before 11pm, the guards threw open the checkpoints and the first Berliners to pass freely from East to West in nearly three decades swarmed across the border. Here, they were met with champagne, joyful hugs and reunited family members, as the ecstatic crowd sang, cheered and climbed on to the wall in celebration. The festival atmosphere surrounding the fall of the Berlin Wall continued well into the next day, as East German army units began dismantling the wall to create more crossing points. Berliners cheered each other on as they attacked the wall with hammers and pickaxes, and took away large chunks as souvenirs. Crowds gathered again that week to watch bulldozers bring down large sections of the wall and reunite ancient Berlin roads.

Today, only a few small sections of the Berlin Wall remain as sightseeing spots for tourists to visit. But few who were there will forget the moment the wall came down, heralding the end of the Cold War and the rapid decline of communist rule in Europe.

A Timeline: the Before, During and After of the Fall of the Berlin Wall

1945 Following the end of the Second World War, Berlin is divided into four sectors: the American, British and French West, and the Soviet East.

June 1946 The Soviet Union insists that the demarcation line between East and West Germany be safeguarded.

October 1946 A 30-day Interzonepass becomes required to travel between East and West Germany.

June 23, 1948 Berlin is divided into two currency zones.

June 23, 1948 The Soviet Union begins the Berlin blockade.

June 24, 1948 The United States starts the Berlin Airlift to keep Berliners supplied with food and fuel.

May 12, 1949 The Soviet Union ends the Berlin blockade.

May 12, 1949 The Federal Republic of Germany (FRG) is founded.

September 1949 The Berlin Airlift ends.

October 7, 1949 The German Democratic Republic (GDR) is founded.

May 26, 1952 The border between East and West Germany is closed, leaving only the border between East and West Berlin open.

December 1957 The GDR government forbids citizens to leave East Germany without permission.

August 13, 1961 The border between East and West Berlin is closed and barriers are erected.

June 1963 American president John F. Kennedy visits Berlin and delivers the words "Ich bin ein Berliner" ("I am a Berliner").

June 12, 1987 President Ronald Reagan visits Berlin and urges Soviet leader Mikhail Gorbachev to dismantle the Berlin Wall.

September 1989 The Hungarian government opens its border with Austria.

November 9, 1989 The Berlin Wall is opened.

October 3, 1990 Germany is reunified.

THE COLLAPSE OF THE SOVIET UNION

1991

"A society should never become like a pond with stagnant water, without movement. That's the most important thing."

Mikhail Gorbachev talks about reforming the Soviet model.

On August 19, 1991, hardline communist members of the government started a military coup by placing Gorbachev under house arrest and issuing an emergency decree that suspended all political activity. As tanks rolled into Moscow, its inhabitants flocked to the Russian parliament building to protect it from attack. Boris Yeltsin, president of the Russian Soviet Federative Socialist Republic (RSFSR), then climbed aboard a tank and implored the soldiers not to fire on the unarmed people of Moscow. As he denounced the coup as an act of terror, his speech was broadcast around the world. It represented the popular will of the Soviet people not to return to a Stalinist society.

On August 20, the military declared a curfew would take effect in Moscow. This was treated as a sign that the military was about to attack the parliament building, the White House. In response, thousands of Moscow citizens began building barricades around the White House and prepared for the tanks to begin firing. However, no attack came that day. Instead, at around 1am the next morning, armored vehicles approached the White House but were unable to pass by the parked buses and cleaning vehicles blocking their way. The military was ordered to retreat: the coup was over.

With the coup over, Gorbachev flew back to Moscow. But here, Boris Yeltsin, the main figure in the resistance to the coup, was already making changes. Although the Russian constitution did not empower the president of the RSFSR with such authority, Yeltsin took advantage of the chaos caused by the coup to push for an end to communist rule. With the support of the people on Yeltsin's side, Gorbachev had little choice but to resign as Communist party secretary. The next day, Yeltsin met with the leaders of Belarus and the Ukraine to announce the end of the Soviet Union.

On December 24, 1991, the Russian Federation informed the United Nations that it would succeed the Soviet Union in its UN membership. None of the member states objected. After the succession of Russia, Gorbachev announced his resignation as Soviet president on December 25. The Soviet flag was lowered from the Kremlin roof and replaced with the new tricolor flag of Russia. What had been the U.S.S.R. became 15 separate countries that agreed to collaborate as the new Commonwealth of Independent States (CIS).

On December 25, 1991, the red hammer-and-sickle flag was lowered from the Kremlin for the last time, as Soviet leader Mikhail Gorbachev resigned. The world looked on in amazement as the Soviet Union officially ended. The collapse had been imminent following an attempted coup by communist hardliners in August, a last-ditch effort to restore party rule to the country and undo Gorbachev's democratic reforms. Gorbachev had inherited a stalled economy when he came to power in 1985 and had instituted the reconstructive policies known as glasnost and perestroika.

Glasnost introduced political openness and did away with Stalinist repression. New freedoms were granted to Soviet citizens, political prisoners were released and newspapers could be critical of government policy. Perestroika brought about economic reform by loosening the government's stranglehold on the economy. For the first time, citizens were allowed to start private businesses, workers were granted the right to strike and foreign investment was encouraged. These new policies brought a profound change, which created breakthrough historical moments such as President Gorbachev and President George H. W. Bush meeting in 1989 to declare the end of the Cold War. However, Gorbachev's new market economy was slow to bear fruit. While the West praised Gorbachev's reforms, his people suffered food shortages at home. As Gorbachev reduced the Soviet military presence among the Warsaw Pact nations of eastern Europe, they too expressed their dissatisfaction. The first revolution took place in Poland, where in 1989 they won the right to hold free elections.

Czechoslovakia was next to overthrow its communist government, and one by one the nations of eastern Europe began to declare their independence from Moscow. In December 1991, Belarus, Russia and the Ukraine entered the Commonwealth of Independent States (CIS) and a few weeks later they were joined by the remaining republics. The Soviet Union had fallen.

A Timeline: the Before, During and After of the Collapse of the Soviet Union

1984 General secretary Yuri Andropov dies and is replaced by Konstantin Chernenko.

1985 Chernenko dies and is replaced by Mikhail Gorbachev as general secretary of the Communist Party.

1986 Gorbachev ends economic aid to Soviet satellite countries.

1987 The U.S. and the Soviet Union agree to scrap intermediate-range nuclear missiles.

1988 Gorbachev replaces Andrei Gromyko as Soviet president.

1989 Gorbachev withdraws Soviet troops from the war against the Taliban in Afghanistan.

August 1989 The solidarity movement in Poland led by Lech Wałęsa wins the right to hold free elections.

November 1989 The Berlin Wall falls.

December 1989 The Velvet Revolution in Czechoslovakia leads to the fall of its communist government.

1990 The U.S.S.R. begins pulling out its military forces from the Warsaw Pact nations.

March 1990 East and West Germany reunite.

March 1990 Boris Yeltsin is elected president of the Russian Soviet Federative Socialist Republic (RSFSR) and leaves the Soviet Communist Party.

July 1991 The Warsaw Pact is dissolved.

August 19, 1991 Senior U.S.S.R. government officials detain Gorbachev at his holiday villa in Crimea and attempt to stage a coup.

August 24, 1991 Yeltsin bans the Soviet Communist Party in Russia, seizes its assets and then recognizes the independence of the Baltic republics.

September 1991 The Congress of People's Deputies votes for the dissolution of the Soviet Union.

December 8, 1991 Leaders of Russia, Ukraine and Belarus sign an agreement setting up the Commonwealth of Independent States (CIS).

December 25, 1991 Gorbachev resigns as Soviet president.

December 26, 1991 The new Russian government takes over the offices of the former U.S.S.R..

Index